Medical Front Line

Kaoru Masago   Hiroaki Tanaka   Bill Benfield

SEIBIDO

音声ファイルのダウンロード/ストリーミング

CD マーク表示がある箇所は、音声を弊社 HP より無料でダウンロード／ストリーミングすることができます。トップページのバナーをクリックし、書籍検索してください。 書籍詳細ページに音声ダウンロードアイコンがございますのでそちらから自習用音声としてご活用ください。

https://www.seibido.co.jp

Medical Front Line

はじめに

　今日，大学教育は講義中心から実習中心，あるいは学習者参加型教育へと大きく変化しています。とりわけ医療英語教育では，アクティブラーニング（Active Learning），スモールグループディスカッション（Small Group discussion），内容を重視した学習（Contents Based Learning）が基礎教養教育から専門教育や実習に至るまで行われています。そこで本書「Medical Front Line」をアクティブラーニングによる英語学習教材として作成しました。本書は，英語による情報の正しい理解に始まり，内容の要約，リサーチからプレゼンテーション訓練もグループで，実習形式で行えるよう教材を工夫しています。グループごとに教え合い，学び合い，伝え合う実践型教育のための教材です。

　本書は 3 つの Chapter と 15 個の Unit で構成されています。Chapter 1 は「生活と健康」というテーマで「医療ボランティア」，「公衆衛生」，「代替医療」，「歯科」などの幅広いテーマを扱いながら，みなさんの生活に身近なトピックを選びました。Chapter 2 は「医療の進歩：私たちが得られる恩恵」というテーマで，最先端の医療の進歩が医療をどのように変えるのかを議論しています。「インフルエンザ」，「糖尿病」，「虫歯」などの比較的身近なトピックから「心臓病」，「敗血症」，「乳がん」，「脳がん」などのやや専門性の高いトピックを扱いました。Chapter 3 は「医療の進歩の裏側」というテーマで最先端の医療技術が進歩する一方で，その弊害やそれに伴う倫理的な問題を扱いました。具体的には，「薬剤」や「生命倫理」です。Chapter 3 では，あえて 2 つの Unit で 1 つのトピックを扱っています。これは積み重ね学習によって深めた理解を基に，ペアやグループで積極的に議論をしてほしいという著者の思いからです。自分自身の意見をしっかりと持ち，英語で発信できるようになってほしいと願っています。

　各 Unit は Vocabulary，Listening，Reading，Writing，Presentation の構成で，総合的に英語力を高められるようになっています。Vocabulary は一般的な英単語と医療英語の両方の習得を目指しています。特に医療英語は発音が難しく，電子辞書でも発音が収録されていない場合があります。本書はすべての単語に発音音声を収録しているので，正しい発音で単語を覚えてください。Listening ではアメリカのニュースの聞き取りにチャレンジします。生の英語なので難易度は高いです。そこでみなさんの学習の助けになるように，スタジオ収録の聞き取りやすい音声も用意しています。ニュースの映像と音声は EnglishCentral という e-learning サイトにアクセスすれば字幕付きで確認することができます。ぜひ活用してください。最後の Writing と Presentation は学習した内容を消化し，それを発信する活動です。巻末には Extra Activities として，グループでの Presentation の活動を 5 つ用意しています。積極的に英語で発言をして，発信する力を磨いてください。

　医療系学生のみなさんは入学以来，その勉強の多さ，重さに驚いていることと思います。新知識の習得や，その習得度確認のための試験，「実習」，最後には「国家試験」も控えています。専門知識に合わせて論理的，批判的「思考能力」や，患者という一般の方々にも分かりやすく説明する「コミュニケーション能力」も求められています。本書は思考力，コミュニケーション力の養成にも役立つ工夫があるので，注目して学習してほしいと思います。

著　者

CONTENTS

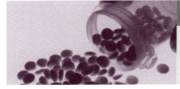

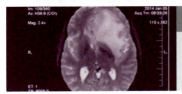

本書の使い方

本書は一般的な 15 回授業以外に 30 回授業にも対応しています。30 回授業では、Extra Activity 1~ 5 をそれぞれ 3 回の授業で学生によるプレゼンテーションを行うことができます。まず一般的な 15 回授業として、各ユニットの学習のねらい、ポイントを示します。

I VOCABULARY

A.：ユニットの語彙のうち、日常的・一般的な語彙を確認します。まず単語と英語の語彙定義を読み、結び合わせてみましょう。わからなくてもまずは推測などで全ての語彙と定義の結び合わせを済ませてください。授業で正解がわかったら、これら A. の語彙は必ず定着させるようにしてください。大学生に必要な語彙でもあります。

B.：医療系の専門語彙が含まれます。また選択肢の用語も医療系専門訳語です。一般の意味とは別に専門用語としての訳もしっかり習得してください。医療従事者としていずれ何度も出会う専門語彙です。

II COMPREHENSION

Step1. Listening Comprehension：教室内で教員の指示に従って DVD 映像を見たり、CD 音声を聞いて、内容を下線に必ず「メモ（文字化）」してください。曖昧な考えやまとまらない内容は「書く」ことでまとまります。日本語でも良いから内容を書いてみましょう。グループ学習では、書いたものを見せ合って比較してください。自分と違ったまとめ方、ポイントが確認できます。ここまでは、**次ページの本文内容を文字で見ないようにしてください。**

Step2. Reading Comprehension：ここからは聞き取れなかった内容が文字で確認できます。T/F 判定は論理的思考の訓練です。T/F の判定の「根拠」を示してください。行目だけでなく、T ならどこと同じ内容か（本文と表現は違っても「同じ内容」であれば T をつけてください）、F なら本文の「どこと、どう違うのか」を論述します。根拠ある論理的な説明は、根拠ある医療 EBM(Evidence Based Medical) に通じます。

Step3. Summary：本文の内容をまとめたものです。空所を埋めながら内容を確認してください。これは内容のダウンサイズ化です。長い内容も元の 1/2、1/3 の長さでまとめる訓練です。長い情報であっても、自分の頭の中で常に「つまり、簡単にまとめると」と考える習慣をつけてください。理系・医療系の人間には必要な訓練です。

III CRITICAL THINKING CHALLENGE

ここからがこのテキストのより重要な学習です。このユニットから「情報を得る」だけでは不十分です。得た情報から、何が問題か、自分はどう考えるか、賛成か反対か、賛成に見えてもさらに補足し、自分なりの、より良いアイデアはないか、これを考えてください。それが「問題解決力」の養成につながります。また情報をそのまま鵜呑みにしない「情報リテラシー」の勉強でもあります。「批判的能力」とは、人のあげあし取りや「非難」ではありません。批判する力は、情報から新しいものを「発見」する創造的な力です。

Step1. まず自分の考えを書き出します。まずは日本語で、できれば Useful Expressions を使い英語で書いてみましょう。

Step2. 個人プレゼンの準備です。自分の意見を「短いプレゼン」と考えて書き出し、スピーチ（発言）のメモとします。小さなスペースですが「まとまった内容を書く」ように努力しましょう。

Step3. (Useful Expressions) 最後に自分の意見を英語で書きます。独創的な表現でなくていいのです。その代り「意見を述べる英語の定型」を使い、その中に自分の考えを「はめ込む」練習もしてください。

e-Learning Exercise

ぜひ、EnglishCentral にアクセスし、News を聞きながら空欄を埋めてください。また Speaking チェックで発音してみてください。教室では案外、個人の発音の機会は少ないものです。ぜひ、自分の発音チェックをして、「英語を発音する時間」を少しでも多く持ってください。

EnglishCentralのご案内

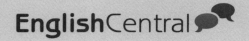

本テキストで学習していただいた動画は、オンライン学習システム「EnglishCentral」で学習することができます。EnglishCentralでは動画の視聴や単語のディクテーションのほか、動画のセリフを音読し録音すると、コンピュータが発音を判定します。PCだけでなく、スマートフォンのアプリからも学習できます。リスニング、スピーキング、語彙力向上のため、ぜひ活用してください。

EnglishCentralの利用にはアカウントとアクセスコードの登録が必要です。登録方法については下記ページにアクセスしてください。

https://www.seibido.co.jp/np/englishcentral/blended.html

見る

本文内でわからなかった単語は1クリックでその場で意味を確認

スロー再生

日英字幕（ON/OFF可）

学ぶ

音声を聴いて空欄の単語をタイピング。ゲーム感覚で楽しく単語を覚える

話す

動画のセリフを音読し録音、コンピュータが発音を判定。

日本人向けに専門開発された音声認識によってスピーキング力を%で判定

ネイティブと自分が録音した発音を聞き比べ練習に生かすことができます

苦手な発音記号を的確に判断し、単語を緑、黄、赤の3色で表示

Chapter 1

生活と健康

Eye Charity Takes Airborne Healing to World

みなさんの身の回りには眼科は当たり前のようにあります。しかし他の国ではどうでしょうか？　この Unit では眼科の医療ボランティアについて学習します。内容に入る前に、眼科の医療ボランティアにはどのような診察、検診、そして治療ができるでしょうか。ペアで話し合ってみましょう。

Ⅰ VOCABULARY

CD 1-2

A. *Match each word with its definition.*

1. income [ ]	**2.** prevent [ ]
3. outfit [ ]	**4.** donate [ ]
5. priority [ ]	

> 選択肢
>
> ア. to provide someone or something with equipment
> イ. monetary payment received for goods or services
> ウ. something given special attention
> エ. to present as a gift, grant, or contribution
> オ. to keep from occurring

B. *Match each medical word with its meaning.*

1. screening [ ]	**2.** operation [ ]
3. surgery [ ]	**4.** surgeon [ ]
5. visually impaired [ ]	**6.** visual impairment [ ]
7. restore [ ]	**8.** blindness [ ]

> 選択肢
>
> ア. 回復する　　イ. 視力障害を患った　　ウ.（外科）手術　　エ.（患部への）手術
> オ. 外科医　　カ. 失明　　キ. 視力障害　　ク. 検査

Ⅱ COMPREHENSION

DVD CD 1-3

 **Step 1** **Listening Comprehension**

Watch the news and discuss the main topic with your partner.

....

....

The world's only Flying Eye Hospital was recently upgraded in a newly outfitted MD-10* aircraft to take medical

workers to countries around the world for screenings and
5 operations . Outside the flying hospital, conditions can be basic.

—*Dr. Daniel Neely, volunteer eye surgeon:*

"You know, you can be in Zambia and the power goes out
10 in the middle of the surgery. You can be there needing to scrub your hands for the surgery and you have to use a bucket of water because the water's gone out."

Partnering with local clinics and hospitals, Orbis* works in Cameroon, Ethiopia, Ghana and Latin America.
15 —*Dr. Jonathan Lord, global medical director, Orbis:*

"You've then got Asia, where we work in China, we work in Vietnam. We have projects running in India, in Bangladesh. We work in Indonesia, so we take the plane wherever our gap analysis, wherever the needs analysis says we can be of help."
20 More than 285 million people around the world are visually impaired, most in low-income countries. Eighty percent of visual impairment problems can be prevented or cured. Among

those helping out are volunteer pilots. Captain Gary Dyson
25 flies cargo planes for FedEx*, but takes time off to fly for Orbis.

—*Captain Gary Dyson, volunteer pilot:*

"When you see a child who can't see on Monday and they
30 can see on Wednesday, you're hooked. You want to see it again and again."

After an operation, the improvement can be dramatic, says a volunteer surgeon.

MD-10／ダグラス社が作る航空機の１種

Orbis／オービス（失明の防止を目的とする国際的な非政府の非営利団体で空飛ぶ眼科を運営している。）

FedEx／フェデックス（物流サービスを提供する会社）

—*Dr. Rosalind Stevens, volunteer surgeon:*

35 "And when we remove the patch the next day, frequently the patient breaks into a big smile."

Orbis provides advanced medical training for local doctors and nurses in an onboard classroom that is linked electronically to the plane's operating room.

40 —*Bob Ranck, Orbis CEO:*

"We teach others to save and restore vision. And we teach health care systems to make it a priority, so the prevalence of blindness in their country will come down."

The newest version of the flying hospital in a plane donated 45 by FedEx will make preliminary flights to several US cities, then head to Shenyang, China in September.

Read the passage and write T if the statement is true or F if it is false. Then, explain with evidence why you chose your answer.

1. Many organizations around the world have their own flying hospitals to help visually impaired people.
   T | F   根拠 [..]

2. Poor economic development is not a factor in the spread of visual impairment.
   T | F   根拠 [..]

3. Visual impairment can be prevented or cured in more than 228 million people.
   T | F   根拠 [..]

4. Pilots voluntarily donate their time and skills to operate the flying hospital around the world including Asia, Africa, South America and Europe.
   T | F   根拠 [..]

5. The Flying Eye Hospital is not just an eye hospital but a teaching facility located on board an aircraft for doctors, nurses, and the public.
   T | F   根拠 [..]

(Step **3**) **Summary**

The following is a brief explanation of the Flying Hospital. Read the passage again and fill in the blanks.

Millions of people (¹   ) from visual impairments because they can't get the (²   ) many of us take for granted. The Flying Eye Hospital is a fully equipped mobile hospital. FedEx has recently (³   ) an MD-10 aircraft and it will be converted into a next-generation, state-of-the-art Flying Eye Hospital. On the outside, the plane is like most other aircraft, but inside, it's like no other — it has an (⁴   ) hospital on board. The flying hospital also (⁵   ) doctors, nurses and technicians to save and (⁶   ) vision. Classrooms are aboard the plane, and local medical personnel are able to watch live surgeries. The Flying Eye Hospital focuses on the prevention of (⁷   ) and the treatment of eye diseases in developing countries.

III **CRITICAL THINKING** CHALLENGE

What's your opinion about the following question?

<u>After graduating from your school, you will become a health care worker such as a doctor, nurse, or pharmacist, etc. What can you do as an international medical volunteer?</u>

<u>Collect information from the Internet and explain your ideas.</u>

Step 1

Exchange ideas with your partner.

Step 2

What do you think? Explain your ideas briefly. You can use expressions from this passage, Summary, or Useful Expressions below.

Step 3

Let's make a presentation.

 Useful Expressions

- I'd like to point out that ～ （～という事を指摘したい）

  例 I'd like to point out that there are many possibilities that you don't notice.

- The question is how we should ～ （問題は私たちがいかに～すべきかだ）

  例 The question is how we should handle cases.

- ～ match one's needs best （～ のニーズに合う）

  例 We must figure out which plans match their needs best.

 e-Learning Exercise

1 Listening
EnglishCentral のサイトにアクセスし、News を聞きながらスクリプトの空欄を埋めなさい。

2 Speaking
EnglishCentral のサイトにアクセスし、Speaking チェックをしなさい。

みなさんは当たり前のように水道水を飲んでいますが、清潔な水は健康に欠かせません。この Unit では浄水の技術について学習します。内容に入る前に、まずは水道水が飲める国が世界でどれぐらいあるのでしょうか？　ペアで話し合ってみましょう。

Ⅰ VOCABULARY

CD 1-5

A. *Match each word with its definition.*

1. efficient	[　　]	**2.** consume	[　　]
3. abundant	[　　]	**4.** improvement	[　　]
5. solution	[　　]		

選択肢

ア. being available in large quantities so that there is more than enough

イ. an act of improving or the state of being improved

ウ. an answer to a problem

エ. working well without wasting time, money or energy

オ. to use time, energy and goods

B. *Match each medical word with its meaning.*

1. filter	[　　]	**2.** filtration	[　　]
3. membrane	[　　]	**4.** layer	[　　]
5. material	[　　]	**6.** molecule	[　　]
7. remove	[　　]	**8.** contaminant	[　　]

選択肢

ア. 取り除く	イ. ろ過する	ウ. ろ過	エ. 膜
オ. 汚染物質	カ. 分子	キ. 層	ク. 物質

Ⅱ COMPREHENSION

DVD CD 1-6

Step 1 Listening Comprehension

Watch the news and discuss the main topic with your partner.

....

....

Developing the perfect water filter is Baoxia Mi's goal. Growing up in China, she learned the value of clean drinking water early on. Now at the University of California, Berkeley, the environmental engineer is developing a new type of
5   membrane that could be more efficient than today's water filtration technology and consume less energy in the process. It's made up of layers of graphene※, 100,000 times thinner than a strand of human hair.

—Baoxia Mi, the
10 *University of California, Berkeley:*

"We made it from graphite※, which is a material that we use in
15 pencils for example, so it's cheap and relatively abundant, so we can use that, and the process that we use to make it from the graphite to the graphene oxide※ is actually quite scalable※."

That means the membranes could be adapted to filter water from a faucet, as well as for large systems used to treat
20 wastewater.

Membranes are much like a maze for water molecules. The water passes through a series of layers separated by spaces specifically designed to remove different types of contaminants.

graphene／グラフェン

graphite／黒鉛・グラファイト

graphene oxide／酸化グラフェン
scalable 拡張可能な

—*Baoxia Mi, the University of California, Berkeley:*

25   "In order to kind of remove different targeted molecules, the most direct way of thinking about it is to control the spacing that we have between the layers."

    The researchers are working on further improvements. They hope their work

30 will contribute to finding solutions to water purification worldwide to make clean water affordable and available

35 for people everywhere.

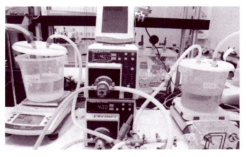

Read the passage and write T if the statement is true or F if it is false. Then, explain with evidence why you chose your answer.

1. Baoxia Mi is a pioneering researcher trying to find a possible solution for purifying impaired water.

    ☐ T ☐ F   根拠 [...]

2. A new kind of graphite discovered by Mi could filter contaminants out of water more effectively than current methods.

    ☐ T ☐ F   根拠 [...]

3. The membrane is specially designed to filter wastewater on an industrial scale.

    ☐ T ☐ F   根拠 [...]

4. The membrane has a complex structure for filtering a wide variety of contaminated materials.

    ☐ T ☐ F   根拠 [...]

5. The layers of graphene are so thin that the spaces between them are impossible to adjust.

    ☐ T ☐ F   根拠 [...]

The following is a short explanation of Baoxia Mi's reseach. Read the passage again and fill in the blanks.

Baoxia Mi, a researcher at the university of California, Berkeley, recognized that clean drinking water was not something to take for granted. She is developing a new type of (1   ) that could outperform today's water filtration technology and consume less (2   ) in the process. Her design is constructed from graphene oxide, a carbon-based material that's made from naturally occurring graphite, the same material found in (3   ). Made from a (4   ) layer of carbon, the material can conduct heat and electricity very well. It's also inexpensive and (5   ). Baoxia says that membranes made from graphene or graphene oxide can more effectively remove wastewater (6   )—including pharmaceuticals, pathogens and endocrine disruptors — than current methods and can be applied to wastewater reuse, water desalinization and storm water treatment.

III **CRITICAL THINKING** CHALLENGE

What's your opinion about the following question?

What is a clean water system using nanotechnology?

Collect information from the Internet and introduce the latest technology.

Step **1**

Exchange ideas with your partner.

Step 2

What do you think? Explain your ideas briefly. You can use expressions from this passage, Summary, or Useful Expressions below.

Step 3

Let's make a presentation.

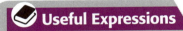 Useful Expressions

- It's really indispensable for us to ～（～することが本当に不可欠である）
  例 It's really indispensable for us to analyze current situations.
- These facts show ～（これらの事実から～が分かる）
  例 These facts show that the skin is the most important system in the body.

 e-Learning Exercise

1 Listening
EnglishCentral のサイトにアクセスし、News を聞きながらスクリプトの空欄を埋めなさい。

2 Speaking
EnglishCentral のサイトにアクセスし、Speaking チェックをしなさい。

UNIT 3
Study: Mindful Meditation Helps Manage Chronic Back Pain

スポーツや重い荷物の持ち運びで腰を痛めた経験はありませんか？　このUnitでは腰痛治療の新しい方法について学習します。内容に入る前に、まずは腰痛の治療といえば、どのような治療が思い浮かびますか？ペアで話し合ってみましょう。

I VOCABULARY

CD 1-8

A. *Match each word with its definition.*

1. alternative [　　]   2. explore [　　]
3. manage [　　]   4. participate [　　]
5. function [　　]

選択肢

ア. to control
イ. to take part in an activity or event
ウ. the kind of action or activity
エ. to investigate, study or analyze
オ. different from the usual or conventional

B. *Match each medical word with its meaning.*

1. prescription [　　]   2. narcotic drug [　　]
3. overdose [　　]   4. pain reliever [　　]
5. addiction [　　]   6. chronic [　　]
7. low back pain [　　]   8. cognitive behavioral therapy [　　]
9. mindfulness [　　]   10. epidemic [　　]

選択肢

ア. 過剰摂取する　イ. 慢性の　ウ. 鎮痛剤　エ. 処方　オ. 認知行動療法
カ. 腰痛　キ. 中毒　ク. (医療用)麻薬　ケ. マインドフルネス　コ. 蔓延・流行

II COMPREHENSION

DVD CD 1-9

Step 1   **Listening Comprehension**

Watch the news and discuss the main topic with your partner.

....

....

The Centers for Disease Control[※] says US prescription narcotic drug use has become a major public health crisis. The CDC says more people than ever are overdosing on prescription pain relievers, and it's fueling an epidemic of heroin[※] addiction,

5 when patients could no longer get prescription opioids[※]. The agency is urging doctors and patients to explore alternative ways to reduce pain. Researchers at the Group Health Research Institute in Seattle, Washington explore the power of the mind .

—*Daniel Cherkin, Group Health Research Institute:*

10 "One of the most important new understandings of chronic pain and chronic low back pain is that the mind plays a very important part."

15 The researchers studied two mind-body therapies. One was cognitive behavioral therapy.

—*Daniel Cherkin, Group Health Research Institute:*

"Cognitive behavioral therapy focuses on helping people learn how to change, how they think their pain, and helps

20 promote concrete activities that people can do to better manage it."

The other therapy is mindfulness, which draws

25 from meditation and yoga.

—*Daniel Cherkin, Group Health Research Institute:*

"Mindfulness tries to help people change their awareness, increase their awareness with their pain and to become more accepting of the pain, and then, to focus their energies on finding

30 ways to constructively manage it."

—*Benjamin Balderson, Group Health Research Institute:*

"We teach things such as how to manage the emotional impact of pain, how to manage the activity impact of pain,

The Centers for Disease Control／アメリカ疾病管理センター、CDC と省略されることが多い。

heroin／ヘロイン（モルヒネから作る鎮痛剤）
opioid／オピオイド（鎮痛作用のある化合物）

how to manage the things that sometimes are not addressed in
35 primary care or in usual care for chronic pain. So, by doing that,
we look at a more holistic level of approach."

More than 300 volunteers, all with back pain, participated
in the study.

—Daniel Cherkin, Group Health Research Institute:

40 "Benefits in decreased pain and improved function lasted
for a full year, which is not common amongst most treatments
for chronic pain."

Cherkin said both mindfulness and cognitive behavioral
therapy could help patients who suffer from other types of
45 chronic pain. The study was published in JAMA — the Journal
of the American Medical Association.

Read the passage and write T if the statement is true or F if it is false. Then, explain with evidence why you chose your answer.

1. Doctors are not allowed to prescribe narcotic drugs because of an epidemic of heroin addiction.
   T   F   根拠 [....]

2. Researchers in Seattle conducted a study focusing on the relationship between pain and psychological factors.
   T   F   根拠 [....]

3. Although cognitive behavioral therapy and mindfulness overlap, cognitive behavioral therapy includes the Buddhist psychological tradition.
   T   F   根拠 [....]

4. Mindfulness-based treatment may prove more effective than cognitive behavioral therapy in easing chronic low back pain.
   T   F   根拠 [....]

5. Quieting the mind could be a non-drug treatment to help decrease chronic low back pain.
   T   F   根拠 [....]

(Step 3) Summary

The following is a short explanation of alternative medication for low back pain. Read the passage again and fill in the blanks.

A team of researchers explored (^{1}) ways to treat chronic pain and chronic low back pain. Researchers addressed a specific kind of (^{2}) called mindfulness along with cognitive behavioral therapy to see if it might (^{3}) pain. Mindfulness therapy was conducted by practicing (^{4}) and yoga. Among volunteers with back pain, treatment using mindfulness and cognitive behavioral therapy resulted in greater (^{5}). These findings suggest that these therapies may be an (^{1}) treatment for patients with chronic pain. Therefore, greater understanding and acceptance of the mind-body connection will provide (^{6}) with new opportunities for improving their lives with chronic back pain.

III CRITICAL THINKING CHALLENGE

What's your opinion about the following question?

Which is more effective for treating chronic pain, treatment with yoga or treatment with pain-killers?

Collect information from the Internet and explain your ideas.

Step 1

Exchange ideas with your partner.

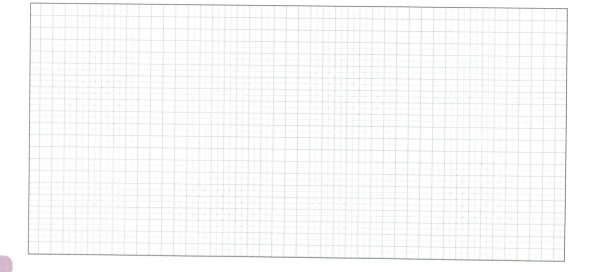

Step 2

What do you think? Explain your ideas briefly. You can use expressions from this passage, Summary, or Useful Expressions below.

Step 3

Let's make a presentation.

Useful Expressions

- In my opinion 〜（私の意見としては、〜）
  例 In my opinion, she shouldn't have done it.

- I personally think that 〜（個人的に〜だと思う）
  例 I personally think that my son is a genius.

- I'm in favor of 〜（〜に賛成である）
  例 I'm in favor of euthanasia.

 e-Learning Exercise

1 Listening

EnglishCentral のサイトにアクセスし、News を聞きながらスクリプトの
空欄を埋めなさい。

2 Speaking

EnglishCentral のサイトにアクセスし、Speaking チェックをしなさい。

UNIT 4

Technology Reduces Time in Dentist's Chair

みなさんは歯医者に行った経験があるでしょう。このUnitでは歯科に取り入れられている技術革新について扱います。内容に入る前に、まずは虫歯を削られたり、詰め物をされた経験を思い出してください。それについて、ペアで話し合ってみましょう。

I VOCABULARY

CD 1-11

A. *Match each word with its definition.*

1. permanent [   ]   2. temporary [   ]
3. instruction [   ]   4. excess [   ]
5. obsolete [   ]

選択肢

ア. no longer useful because something newer and better has been invented
イ. a statement telling someone what they must do
ウ. additional and not needed because there is already enough of something
エ. continuing for only a limited period of time
オ. continuing to exist for a long time

B. *Match each medical word with its meaning.*

1. medical instrument [   ]   2. tooth crown [   ]
3. drilling [   ]   4. insert [   ]
5. grind [   ]   6. cement [   ]
7. genetic engineering [   ]   8. cloning [   ]

選択肢

ア. 接着する   イ. 粉砕する   ウ. 挿入する   エ. 切削（せっさく）
オ. 歯冠   カ. 医療機器   キ. クローン作製   ク. 遺伝子工学

II COMPREHENSION

DVD CD 1-12

Step 1   **Listening Comprehension**

Watch the news and discuss the main topic with your partner.

....
....

Computer-aided medical instruments are increasingly making life easier for doctors and their patients. It used to be that the common but complicated procedure to get a tooth crown required several visits to the dentist's office. While a
5 dental technician※ was preparing the permanent replacement for a damaged tooth, the patient had to wear a temporary crown. Since the mid-1980s, this procedure has gradually been taken

over by robotic machines that reduce the job to just
10 over two hours. Sitting in the dentist's chair takes even less time.

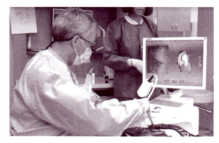

—*Michael Silveus, dentist:*

"It's about 12 minutes' worth of chair time for the patient
15 and, the rest of the time, it's work that's taking place outside the patient's mouth."

At his dental office in Northern Virginia, close to Washington, Michael Silveus and his assistant prepare a patient's tooth for a new crown. The actual drilling takes about
20 five minutes. Instead of making the impression of the damaged tooth in a plastic material, Silveus uses a wand※ with a video camera to scan the tooth and the surrounding area. At this point the computer takes over, designing the new crown and creating instructions for a robotic milling machine. A porcelain cube※,
25 no larger than the tooth, is inserted between two precise drills, similar to the dentist's drill, that grind away excess material, turning the cube into a perfectly matching tooth crown. To harden, the crown must be baked※ at high temperature for about

ten minutes. During that
30 process, it also gets tinted※ to match the color of the neighboring teeth, so it is ready to be cemented in the

dental technician／歯科技工士

wand／細い棒

porcelain cube／陶材製のキューブ

bake／焼く

tint／色合いをつける

patient's mouth.

35　　Patients are pleased with the result.

—*Patient:*

　　"It feels amazing. The tooth feels like my tooth."

　　Dr. Silveus says even this technology may someday become obsolete.

40　—*Michael Silveus, dentist:*

　　"The other thing we look forward to is genetic engineering and eventually cloning, so you can make the crown out of actually enamel, just like the patient's natural teeth are."

　　But for now, he says, his patients are happy to be able to

45　get a new crown in just one visit.

Read the passage and write T if the statement is true or F if it is false. Then, explain with evidence why you chose your answer.

1. The drilling of a decayed tooth has gradually been displaced by robotic machines.

　　| T | F |　根拠　[....]

2. The new technology for crowning a tooth does not require drilling.

　　| T | F |　根拠　[....]

3. A small scanning device is used to take digital pictures inside the mouth.

　　| T | F |　根拠　[....]

4. The porcelain tooth crown is baked and stained in a clinic for a realistic finish.

　　| T | F |　根拠　[....]

5. Dr. Silveus believes porcelain cubes will no longer be needed for making tooth crowns in a few years because of advances in genetic and cloning technology.

　　| T | F |　根拠　[....]

 **Summary** 1-13

The following is a short explanation of the new technology for dentists. Read the passage again and fill in the blanks.

A new computer-aided medical instrument requires (^{1}) time in the dental chair, resulting in (^{1}) discomfort and achieving satisfying results. The process of crowning a tooth starts out with (^{2}). Then, instead of making a mold and sending it to a lab to prepare the (^{3}) replacement for a damaged tooth, dentists are now using a small camera to (^{4}) teeth directly. The digitized image is then sent to an on-site robotic milling machine that (^{5}) away excess material and carves the crown from a porcelain cube. After about 15 minutes of preparation the crown is ready to be (^{6}) in the patient's mouth. Patients don't need to visit the dentist several times anymore.

III CRITICAL THINKING CHALLENGE

What's your opinion about the following question?

Do you know about 3D printers?

Collect information from the Internet on 3D printers and dental treatment and explain it.

Step 1

Exchange ideas with your partner.

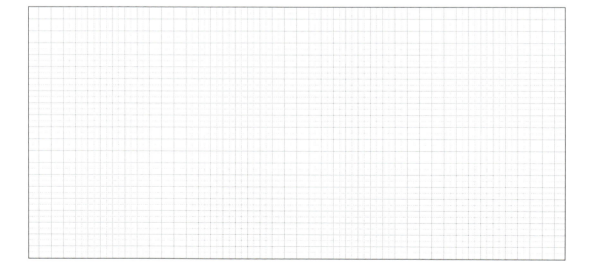

Step 2

What do you think? Explain your ideas briefly. You can use expressions from this passage, Summary, or Useful Expressions below.

Step 3

Let's make a presentation.

📖 Useful Expressions

- To what degree do you think ～ realistic?（～はどの程度現実的だと思いますか？）
  例 To what degree do you think their plan is realistic?

- I will give you an overview of ～（～について概略を述べます）
  例 I will give you an overview of how the CO_2 system works.

- I am going to talk about the status of ～（～の状況について話します）
  例 I am going to talk about the current status of the economy.

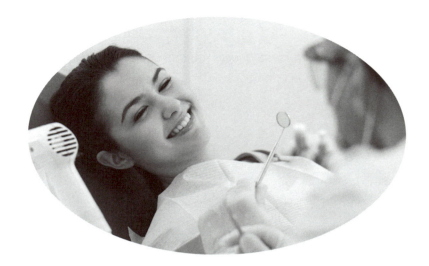

 e-Learning Exercise

1 Listening
EnglishCentral のサイトにアクセスし、News を聞きながらスクリプトの空欄を埋めなさい。

2 Speaking
EnglishCentral のサイトにアクセスし、Speaking チェックをしなさい。

Chapter 2

医療の進歩：私たちが得られる恩恵

Study: Flu Shots Keep People out of Hospital

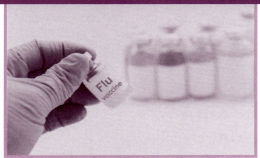

> インフルエンザは毎年のように流行を繰り返すウイルス性の急性感染症で、日本でも毎年死者がでます。日本では何人の死者が毎年出ているでしょうか？　内容に入る前に、ペアで考えてみましょう。

I VOCABULARY

CD 1-14

A. *Match each word with its definition.*

1. concerned [ ]
2. effective [ ]
3. individual [ ]
4. recommend [ ]
5. frequent [ ]

選択肢

ア. successful and working in the way that was intended
イ. to advise someone to do something
ウ. being worried about something
エ. doing something often
オ. a person

B. *Match each medical word with its meaning.*

1. influenza (flu) [ ]
2. be hospitalized [ ]
3. complication [ ]
4. pneumonia [ ]
5. vaccinate [ ]
6. vaccine [ ]
7. immune system [ ]
8. hygiene [ ]

選択肢

| ア. 入院する | イ. 予防接種する | ウ. インフルエンザ | エ. 肺炎 |
| オ. 免疫システム | カ. 衛生 | キ. ワクチン | ク. 合併症 |

II COMPREHENSION

DVD CD 1-15

Step 1 Listening Comprehension

Watch the news and discuss the main topic with your partner.

....

....

We asked America's top public health specialist[※] what he is most concerned about, and this is what he said.

—Dr. Tom Frieden, director, US Centers for Disease Control and Prevention:

5   "Influenza remains the largest single risk the world faces."

Even in a good year, when the flu is relatively mild, hundreds of thousands of people die from flu around the world.

—Dr. Tom Frieden, director, US Centers for Disease Control and Prevention:

10   "And in a bad flu year, it goes into the millions."

The Centers for Disease Control, or the CDC, says in the US, more than 200,000

15 people are hospitalized from flu-related complications each year. Pneumonia is one of the most serious complications of the flu. A new study looked at thousands of patients with pneumonia who were admitted to US hospitals[※] over three flu seasons.

—Dr. Carlos Grijalva, Vanderbilt University Medical Center:

20   "About six percent of those patients had pneumonia due to influenza."

The researchers also looked at how many patients with
25 pneumonia had been vaccinated against the flu.

—Dr. Kathryn Edwards, Vanderbilt University Medical Center:

"The people that had received vaccine had 57 percent less chance of getting hospitalized with flu pneumonia than those
30 patients that were not vaccinated."

The researchers found the vaccines were a little less effective for older patients and for those who have weakened immune systems.

—Dr. Kathryn Edwards, Vanderbilt University Medical Center:

35 "The vaccine seemed to work very well in young children and individuals less than 65."

Because the vaccine 40 isn't 100 percent effective, doctors also recommend good hygiene, frequent hand washing, and staying away from those who have the flu. The study appears in JAMA — the Journal of the American Medical Association.

Read the passage and write T if the statement is true or F if it is false. Then, explain with evidence why you chose your answer.

1. According to America's top public health specialist, influenza is still the most dangerous disease in the world.

[T | F] 　根拠　[....]

2. More than 200,000 people are admitted to hospital due to influenza-related pneumonia.

[T | F] 　根拠　[....]

3. The influenza vaccination can prevent more than half of patients from being hospitalized with pneumonia.

[T | F] 　根拠　[....]

4. Vaccination provides strong protection against influenza infections in healthy adults aged 70 or above.

[T | F] 　根拠　[....]

5. Good health habits like washing hands are a more effective strategy for preventing infections than vaccination.

[T | F] 　根拠　[....]

(Step 3) Summary

The following is a short explanation of influenza and flu-related pneumonia. Read the passage again and fill in the blanks.

(^{1}) remains an important cause of death worldwide. In the United States, (^{2}) from seasonal influenza epidemics are responsible for more than 200,000 hospitalizations. (^{3}), the leading infectious cause of hospitalization and death in the United States, is a serious complication of influenza. A new study looked at thousands of patients with flu-related pneumonia and evaluated the relationship between influenza (^{4}) and pneumonia. The result suggests the flu (^{4}) could (^{5}) not only influenza but pneumonia as well. The investigators also noted that the effectiveness of influenza vaccination for preventing pneumonia hospitalization seemed (^{6}) for young children and individuals less than 65, but lower for older adults and for patients with a weakened (^{7}) system.

III CRITICAL THINKING CHALLENGE

What's your opinion about the following question?

<u>Which is more important, vaccination or good hygiene?</u>
<u>Collect information from the Internet and explain your ideas.</u>

Step 1

Exchange ideas with your partner.

Step 2

What do you think? Explain your ideas briefly. You can use expressions from this passage, Summary, or Useful Expressions below.

Step 3

Let's make a presentation.

 Useful Expressions

- I support the idea of 〜 （〜の考えを支持する）

  例 I support the idea of the death penalty.

- 〜 has more advantages than disadvantages （〜はマイナス面よりプラス面の方が多い）

  例 Using the Internet has more advantages than disadvantages.

- I can't support the idea because 〜 （私はその考えを支持できない。なぜなら〜）

  例 I can't support the idea because the evidence is not reliable enough.

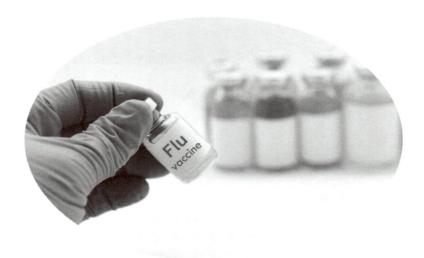

 e-Learning Exercise

1 Listening

EnglishCentral のサイトにアクセスし、News を聞きながらスクリプトの空欄を埋めなさい。

2 Speaking

EnglishCentral のサイトにアクセスし、Speaking チェックをしなさい。

Simple New Test Detects Early Signs of Diabetes

糖尿病とは血糖値が病的に高い状態を指す病名です。写真は血糖値を測定する代表的な装置です。どのように測定しているのでしょうか？　本文の内容に入る前に、ペアで意見交換してみましょう。

I VOCABULARY

CD 1-17

A. *Match each word with its definition.*

1. estimate [　　] 2. contain [　　]
3. measure [　　] 4. measurement [　　]
5. available [　　]

選択肢

ア. to have within
イ. to discover the exact size or amount of something
ウ. to form an approximate judgement regarding the amount or size
エ. present and ready for use
オ. the act or process of measuring something

B. *Match each medical word with its meaning.*

1. diabetes [　　] 2. autoimmune disease [　　]
3. lethal [　　] 4. untreated [　　]
5. side effect [　　] 6. chemical [　　]
7. compound [　　] 8. diagnosis [　　]

選択肢

ア. 致命的な　　イ. 化学物質　　ウ. 糖尿病　　エ. 自己免疫疾患
オ. 診断　　カ. 副作用、副次的影響　　キ. 治療しないまま　　ク. 化合物

II COMPREHENSION

DVD CD 1-18

(Step **1**) **Listening Comprehension**

Watch the news and discuss the main topic with your partner.

....

....

It is estimated that each year, as many as 80,000 children develop Type 1 diabetes※. The autoimmune disease can be lethal if untreated, so early discovery is of ultimate importance. One of the side effects of diabetes is sweet-smelling breath. Oxford
5　University Emeritus Professor of Chemistry Gus Hancock says it is due to the build-up of chemicals called ketones※ in the patient's blood.

—Gus Hancock, Oxford University:

"The sweet smell is this particular ketone which is given
10　out; it's called acetone※. And doctors have regularly smelled acetone on the breath of patients who are in a state of diabetic ketoacidosis※ and used it as a diagnostic."

British researchers say they have developed a portable breath analyzer that can detect even a very small amount of
15　acetone in the patient's breath. CEO※ of Oxford Medical Diagnostics, Ian Campbell, says it was not an easy task, because breath contains molecules of millions of compounds while
20　this test requires detecting only one of them.

—Ian Campbell, Oxford Medical Diagnostics:

"What we do is we allow the subject to blow into the device, we extract out the volatile organic compound※ we wish
25　to measure, in this case acetone. The remainder of the breath passes through the device. We then release the molecules that we're interested in into the cavity to make the measurement."

Professor Hancock, who collaborated in the development of the device, says similar analyzers exist but only as desktop-
30　sized heavy boxes.

—Gus Hancock, Oxford University:

"The aim that we have is to get this into a hand-held device, here, that somebody can pick up and use by blowing simply

Type 1 diabetes 1 型糖尿病（糖尿病は血糖値が病的に高い状態をさす病名で、1 型糖尿病は児童期に発症することが多い。）

ketone／ケトン

acetone／アセトン

diabetic ketoacidosis／糖尿病性ケトアシドーシス（1 型糖尿病に起こる合併症の 1 つ。）

CEO／最高経営責任者

volatile organic compound／揮発性有機化合物

through a mouth-piece."

35   Researchers say the new analyzer should be ready for doctors' offices within a year, while even smaller versions 40 for individual use may be available later. But

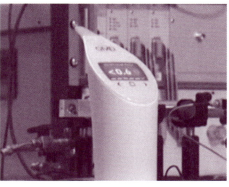

they point out the breath analyzer should be seen only as a first screening, and a diagnosis must be confirmed by a proper blood test.

Read the passage and write T if the statement is true or F if it is false. Then, explain with evidence why you chose your answer.

1. No fewer than 80,000 children are diagnosed with Type 1 diabetes annually.

   | T | F | | 根拠 | [....]

2. The sweet-smelling breath in a diabetic patient is a side effect of treatment drugs.

   | T | F | | 根拠 | [....]

3. Gus Hancock is the first man who invented the device for measuring acetone in diabetic patients' breath.

   | T | F | | 根拠 | [....]

4. The new analyzer is small enough to be used or operated while being held in the hand.

   | T | F | | 根拠 | [....]

5. Doctors can easily make a definite diagnosis of diabetes by using the new analyzer.

   | T | F | | 根拠 | [....]

(**Step 3**) **Summary**

The following is a short explanation of the breath analyzer. Read the passage again and fill in the blanks.

It is thought that 80,000 children develop Type 1 diabetes each year. The researchers are working on the (¹   ) of a small hand-held device that would allow the possibility of breath measurements for (²   ), which can be a marker of Type 1 diabetes. This simple breath test may (³   ) doctors to make a diagnosis quickly and noninvasively. But the invention of the device is not (⁴   ) because breath (⁵   ) molecules of many compounds that can throw results off. Currently, testing for diabetes requires a (⁶   ) test.

III CRITICAL THINKING CHALLENGE

What's your opinion about the following question?

Which is more important for examinations, practicability or precision?

Collect information from the Internet and explain your ideas.

Step 1

Exchange ideas with your partner.

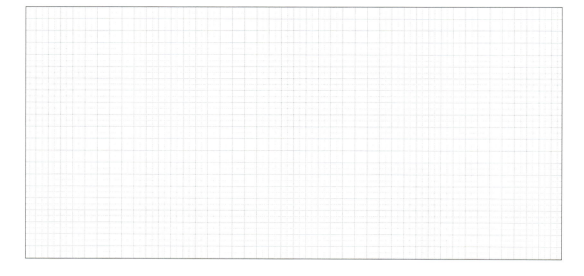

Step 2

What do you think? Explain your ideas briefly. You can use expressions from this passage, Summary, or Useful Expressions below.

Step 3

Let's make a presentation.

 Useful Expressions

- The consensus is that 〜 （一致した意見は〜である）

  例 The consensus is that the patient should wear the eyepatch.

- There are advantages and disadvantages to 〜 （〜にはメリットとデメリットがある）

  例 There are advantages and disadvantages to having your own website.

- We have to think about 〜 （〜について考えなければならない）

  例 We have to think about our future seriously.

 e-Learning Exercise

1 Listening

EnglishCentral のサイトにアクセスし、News を聞きながらスクリプトの空欄を埋めなさい。

2 Speaking

EnglishCentral のサイトにアクセスし、Speaking チェックをしなさい。

UNIT 7

Technique May Eliminate Drill-and-Fill Dental Care

歯医者で虫歯の治療をする時に、歯を削られた経験があるでしょう。削る作業にはしばしば患者の不快感や痛みが伴います。では虫歯を削らずに治すことは可能でしょうか？内容に入る前に、ペアで考えてみましょう。

Ⅰ VOCABULARY

CD 1-20

A. *Match each word with its definition.*

1. periodically   [   ]   2. replacement   [   ]
3. deposit   [   ]   4. routine   [   ]
5. essential   [   ]

選択肢

ア. at regular intervals of time
イ. happening as a normal part of a job or process
ウ. to put something down in a particular place
エ. extremely important and necessary
オ. substitution of an item with a similar or different one

B. *Match each medical word with its meaning.*

1. cavity   [   ]   2. decayed   [   ]
3. tissue   [   ]   4. filling   [   ]
5. enamel   [   ]   6. bacteria   [   ]
7. remineralization   [   ]   8. injection   [   ]

選択肢

| ア. 虫歯になった | イ. 虫歯 | ウ. 注射 | エ. 再石灰化 |
| オ. 充填・歯の詰め物 | カ. 細菌・バクテリア | キ. 組織 | ク. エナメル |

Ⅱ COMPREHENSION

DVD CD 1-21

Step 1 **Listening Comprehension**

Watch the news and discuss the main topic with your partner.

....

....

For over 100 years, dentists have been repairing cavities by removing the decayed tooth tissue with a drill and filling the hole with metal or plastic material. Depending on the

5 cavity's depth, this method can be unpleasant to downright※ painful for the patient, and it has to be repeated periodically.

downright／本当に・完全に

—Rebecca Moazzez, senior lecturer at King's College:

10 "You're really in that cycle of repair and replacement for the rest of the tooth's life."

A damaged tooth's enamel can be replaced naturally, but the process is too slow to stop

15 the work of bacteria that build

Rebecca Moazzez
SENIOR LECTURER AT KING'S COLLEGE

up in tiny cracks. A British company called Reminova※ has developed a method for speeding up this natural remineralization of early-stage cavities.

Reminova／レミノーバ

—Jeff Wright, CEO of Reminova:

20 "We've just found a way to make that a much faster process, driving healthy calcium and phosphate※ minerals into your enamel, and through a natural process, it will bind on and add to the enamel that's

25 there."

phosphate／リン酸塩

After cleaning the cavity with a method that does not require drilling, the dentist covers it with a mineral solution※ and applies an electrical current too weak for the patient to feel.

30 The deposited mineral quickly hardens, completely filling the cavity. Researchers say this method could be especially useful for children.

solution／溶液

42

—Barry Quinn, consultant at King's College:

35 "If children have a better experience of going to the dentist, so they haven't had necessary drilling and injections for routine fillings, then they'll be much more positive in later life and probably become much more regular patients."

Dentists point out that the new method is most efficient on early-stage cavities, which makes regular dental checkups 40 essential. The whole treatment lasts about as long as a regular drill-and-fill procedure. The researchers say they are confident that the new method can be further developed for treating later-stage cavities. And they remind us that regular brushing with fluoride toothpaste helps prevent cavities in the first place.

Read the passage and write T if the statement is true or F if it is false. Then, explain with evidence why you chose your answer.

1. Removing the decayed tooth tissue with a drill and filling the hole is always uncomfortable for a patient.

　T　│　F　│　**根 拠**　[....]

2. Remineralization is a naturally occurring process in which a damaged tooth's enamel is repaired.

　T　│　F　│　**根 拠**　[....]

3. Barry Quinn thinks this technology will help dentists to obtain regular patients.

　T　│　F　│　**根 拠**　[....]

4. Treatment using Reminova's new technology is much faster than conventional treatment.

　T　│　F　│　**根 拠**　[....]

5. The new treatment allows people to spend less time on regular tooth brushing and cleaning.

　T　│　F　│　**根 拠**　[....]

(Step 3) Summary

The following is a short explanation of the new dental technology. Read the passage again and fill in the blanks.

(¹   ) and filling is one of the most (²   ) procedures carried out by dentists. But a new technology could dramatically (³   ) the need for the unpleasant treatment. The company Reminova has invented a way to greatly accelerate the natural remineralization process in tooth (⁴   ). First, the cavity with decayed tissue is gently cleaned without using a (¹   ) method. Then, an electrical current is used that is too (⁵   ) to cause any physical sensation in the patient, to help accelerate mineral ions back into the tooth enamel, rebuilding the mineral levels to normal healthy levels. No healthy tooth tissue is removed in this treatment, and consequently there is no need for (⁶   ) and (¹   ), making for a much less (⁷   ) and a safer experience for patients. The result is repaired natural enamel.

Ⅲ CRITICAL THINKING CHALLENGE

What's your opinion about the following question?

Which is more important, treatment with the latest technology or preventive care?

Collect information from the Internet and explain your ideas.

Step 1

Exchange ideas with your partner.

Step 2

What do you think? Explain your ideas briefly. You can use expressions from this passage, Summary, or Useful Expressions below.

Step 3

Let's make a presentation.

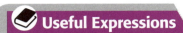 **Useful Expressions**

- We have to be more careful dealing with 〜（〜を取り扱うには、より注意を払う必要がある）

  例 We have to be more careful dealing with the problem.

- As far as I'm concerned 〜（私に関する限り〜、私の考えでは〜）

  例 As far as I'm concerned, it's man-made climate change.

 e-Learning Exercise

1 Listening

EnglishCentral のサイトにアクセスし、News を聞きながらスクリプトの空欄を埋めなさい。

2 Speaking

EnglishCentral のサイトにアクセスし、Speaking チェックをしなさい。

Revolutionary Cardiac Patch Could Mend a Broken Heart

医師が患者の患部に遠隔で治療ができるとしたらどうでしょうか？　そのような技術革新で治療が行えるのはどの臓器だと思いますか？　内容に入る前に、ペアで相談してみましょう。

I VOCABULARY

CD 1-23

A. *Match each word with its definition.*

1. lab [　]	**2.** alert [　]
3. immediately [　]	**4.** stimulation [　]
5. permanently [　]	

選択肢

ア. a special room or building in which a scientist does tests or prepares substances

イ. to make someone realize something important or dangerous

ウ. an action or thing that causes someone or something to become more active

エ. without delay

オ. for a very long time

B. *Match each medical word with its meaning.*

1. activate [　]	**2.** medication [　]
3. cardiac muscle [　]	**4.** regenerate [　]
5. defective [　]	**6.** physician [　]
7. transplant [　]	**8.** organ [　]

選択肢

ア. 活性化させる	イ. 再生する	ウ. 欠陥のある	エ. 臓器
オ. 薬剤	カ. 医師	キ. 移植	ク. 心筋

II COMPREHENSION

 DVD CD 1-24

Step 1 Listening Comprehension

Watch the news and discuss the main topic with your partner.

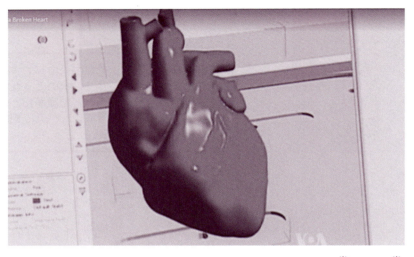

Researchers have developed a 3D-printed* patch*, consisting of live heart tissue grown in a lab and nano-electronics.

—*Tal Dvir, professor, Tel Aviv University:*

5 "The role of the electronics is to sense the function of the tissue and to provide or activate the tissue when needed."

Besides releasing medication, the device could make it possible for the cardiac muscle to regenerate by building up 10 cells in the defective part of the heart. The device could alert the doctor from afar* about the patient's condition.

—*Tal Dvir, professor, Tel Aviv University:*

15 "The patient sitting in his house is not feeling well, and the physician immediately sees the condition of the heart on his computer, and can remotely activate the heart, can provide electrical stimulation, can release drugs."

For a heart permanently damaged by disease or a heart 20 attack, the patch could become an alternative to a heart transplant. And it may lead to even more promising discoveries.

3D-print／3D 印刷する
patch／パッチ

afar／遠方

—Tal Dvir, professor, Tel Aviv University:

"We are trying to 3D-print the whole organ, the whole
25 heart, with the electronics within. And I believe that in the future, in 10-20 years, there would be such bionic organs in the market or in hospitals to be transplanted."

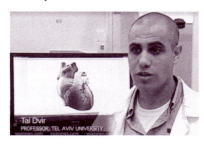

30 The heart patch still needs to be tested, and it could be years before it's available.

Read the passage and write T if the statement is true or F if it is false. Then, explain with evidence why you chose your answer.

1. The bionic heart patch integrates both organic parts and engineered elements that could allow doctors to monitor patients' heart function.

T   F   根拠 [....]

2. The bionic heart patch cannot treat damaged heart tissue.

T   F   根拠 [....]

3. The technology provides remote monitoring, electrical stimulation, and the automatic release of medication.

T   F   根拠 [....]

4. For patients whose hearts have been damaged, the patch could be a revolutionary substitute for heart transplants.

T   F   根拠 [....]

5. The researcher is hopeful that artificial organs can be created for transplantation.

T   F   根拠 [....]

The following is a short explanation of the cardiac patch. Read the passage again and fill in the blanks.

The researchers created an innovative heart patch to develop functional substitutes for tissue permanently ([1]   ) by heart attacks and cardiac disease. The nanotechnological tool combines both living tissue and electronic components to replace the damaged parts of the organ. The patch not only replaces organic tissue but also ensures its sound functioning through remote monitoring. The electronic components allow physicians to ([2]   ) monitor their patients' condition whether they are in the hospital or at home. A physician just logs into a computer and can see if the patient is feeling well. If something seems to be wrong with the patient's heart, the physician can provide electrical ([3]   ) or ([4]   ) drugs. The practical realization of the technology may take some ([5]   ), but it may lead to even more promising discoveries such as creating ([6]   ) organs.

III CRITICAL THINKING CHALLENGE

What's your opinion about the following question?

What is one of the latest technologies for treating heart disease?
Collect information from the Internet and explain your ideas.

Step 1

Exchange ideas with your partner.

Step 2

What do you think? Explain your ideas briefly. You can use expressions from this passage, Summary, or Useful Expressions below.

Step 3

Let's make a presentation.

 Useful Expressions

- What I'd like to stress is that 〜 （私が強調したいのは〜である）
  例 What I'd like to stress is that you should be aware of environmental problems.

- The best alternative is to 〜 （最善の代替案は〜である）
  例 The best alternative is to develop a pharmaceutical distribution network.

 e-Learning Exercise

1 Listening

EnglishCentral のサイトにアクセスし、News を聞きながらスクリプトの
空欄を埋めなさい。

2 Speaking

EnglishCentral のサイトにアクセスし、Speaking チェックをしなさい。

UNIT 9
New Deadly Septic Shock Treatment Could Save Millions

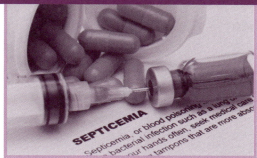

敗血症という病気を聞いたことがあります
か？ 敗血症は、血液中に細菌やウイルス、
真菌が侵入することで起こります。では、
日本での敗血症の死亡率はどれぐらいだと
思いますか？ 内容に入る前に、ペアで相
談してみましょう。

I VOCABULARY

CD 1-26

A. *Match each word with its definition.*

1. confusion 　　　　[　]
2. trigger 　　　　[　]
3. absorb 　　　　[　]
4. capture 　　　　[　]
5. phase 　　　　[　]

> 選択肢
>
> ア. to catch something
> イ. to make something happen
> ウ. to take in liquid, gas, or another substance
> エ. one of the stages of a process
> オ. a situation in which people are uncertain about what to do

B. *Match each medical word with its meaning.*

1. sepsis 　　　　[　]
2. inflammation 　　　　[　]
3. inflammatory 　　　　[　]
4. blood pressure 　　　　[　]
5. pathogen 　　　　[　]
6. cell wall 　　　　[　]
7. fungus 　　　　[　]
8. infected 　　　　[　]

> 選択肢
>
> ア. 菌　　　イ. 炎症性の　　　ウ. 敗血症　　　エ. 細胞壁
> オ. 炎症　　カ. 病原体　　　キ. 感染した　　　ク. 血圧

II COMPREHENSION

DVD CD 1-27

(Step 1) Listening Comprehension

Watch the news and discuss the main topic with your partner.

Sepsis can be triggered by pneumonia, surgery, even childbirth. Symptoms include fever, increased breathing, and confusion. The body's defense system goes out of control, causing widespread inflammation, organ failure* and septic
5　shock*, where blood pressure drops to a dangerously low level. Scientists at Harvard University's Wyss Institute are working on a new dialysis system* that cleans the blood of poisonous pathogens before they trigger that deadly inflammatory response*.

10　—*Mike Super, senior scientist:*

"The current standard of therapy is to give antibiotics and fluids, but what we are talking about here is treatment
15　for sepsis."

The researchers are filtering* blood through a tube with tiny mesh fibers coated with an engineered protein called fcMBL.

—*Mike Super, senior scientist:*

20　"They bind the cell wall of bacteria, of fungi, of many viruses, of many parasites and they bind the toxins as well."

Mike Super describes the procedure.

organ failure／臓器不全

septic shock／敗血症性ショック

dialysis system／透析装置
inflammatory response／炎症反応

filter／ろ過する

—Mike Super, senior scientist:

"We're coating the inside of the tubes with that protein and
25 then we are running the infected blood from the patient through
that, through the filter and binding, absorbing, capturing the
pathogens that are in that
blood, so that the blood
that is going back to the
30 patient after the dialysis is
cleansed."

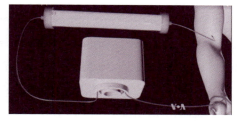

In a trial phase using rats, the dialysis treatment was more
than 99 percent effective in filtering out deadly bacteria. The
research team hopes to begin human trials soon, in hopes of
35 saving many lives around the world.

Read the passage and write T if the statement is true or F if it is false. Then, explain with evidence why you chose your answer.

1. Sepsis is a serious disease that causes respiratory infections such as pneumonia.

　T　F　　根 拠　[....]

2. For patients with sepsis, their immune system becomes uncontrollable, and this can lead to serious conditions like organ failure.

　T　F　　根 拠　[....]

3. The administration of fluids and antibiotics is a basic therapy for patients with sepsis.

　T　F　　根 拠　[....]

4. Mike Super's special weapon for sepsis treatment is an engineered protein called fcMBL.

　T　F　　根 拠　[....]

5. The innovative system described in this passage is more than 99 percent effective in filtering out deadly bacteria in patients' blood.

　T　F　　根 拠　[....]

(Step 3) Summary

The following is a short explanation of the new technology for treating sepsis. Read the passage again and fill in the blanks.

Sepsis is a deadly immune response triggered by infection, which can cause widespread ([1]   ), blood clotting, organ failure, and death. It can ([2]   ) from ([3]   ), surgery and even childbirth. A new device developed by Mike Super and his colleagues may radically transform the way doctors ([4]   ) sepsis. The device is able to cleanse human blood tested in the laboratory and increase survival in rats with infected blood. It can filter live and dead ([5]   ) from the blood, as well as dangerous toxins that are released from the pathogens. The researchers hope to start human ([6]   ) in the near future.

III CRITICAL THINKING CHALLENGE

What's your opinion about the following question?

What is sepsis?

Collect information from the Internet and explain it.

Step 1

Exchange ideas with your partner.

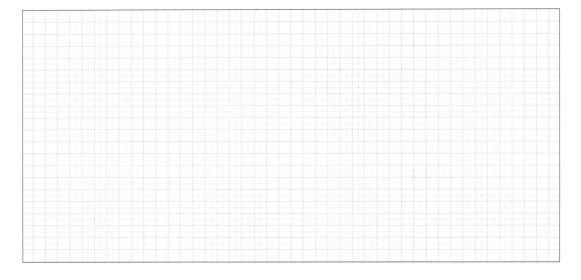

Step 2

What do you think? Explain your ideas briefly. You can use expressions from this passage, Summary, or Useful Expressions below.

Step 3

Let's make a presentation.

 **Useful Expressions**

- The fact is that 〜 （事実は〜である）

  例 **The fact is that** she is ill.

- In a similar vein （同様に）

  例 **In a similar vein**, there are many studies that address the problems.

- When it comes to 〜 （〜と言えば）

  例 **When it comes to fishing**, he's an expert.

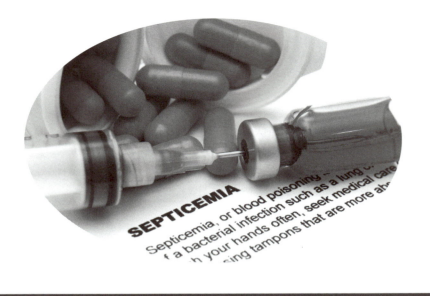

 e-Learning Exercise

1 Listening

EnglishCentral のサイトにアクセスし、News を聞きながらスクリプトの空欄を埋めなさい。

2 Speaking

EnglishCentral のサイトにアクセスし、Speaking チェックをしなさい。

Targeted Treatment May Improve Odds for Breast Cancer Patients

> がんを治療するには適切な抗がん剤を選ぶ必要があります。この Unit では乳がんの抗がん剤治療を扱います。内容に入る前に、日本で乳がんの患者数はどれぐらいでしょうか？　ペアで考えてみましょう。

I VOCABULARY

CD 1-29

A. *Match each word with its definition.*

1. complete   [   ]   **2.** eliminate   [   ]

3. survival   [   ]   **4.** predict   [   ]

5. automatically   [   ]

> 選択肢
>
> ア. to declare or tell in advance
> イ. the state of continuing to live or exist
> ウ. without thinking about what you are doing
> エ. used to emphasize that situation is as great as it could possibly be
> オ. to completely get rid of something that is unnecessary or unwanted

B. *Match each medical word with its meaning.*

1. breast cancer   [   ]   **2.** cancerous   [   ]

3. toxic   [   ]   **4.** toxicity   [   ]

5. tumor   [   ]   **6.** petri dish   [   ]

7. microscopic   [   ]   **8.** fluorescent   [   ]

> 選択肢
>
> ア. 毒性   イ. 腫瘍   ウ. 乳がん   エ. 有害な
> オ. がん性の   カ. 蛍光性の   キ. 微小な   ク. シャーレ

II COMPREHENSION

DVD CD 1-30

(Step 1) **Listening Comprehension**

Watch the news and discuss the main topic with your partner.

....

....

When Shante Thomas was first diagnosed with Stage 2 breast cancer, it came as a complete shock.

—Shante Thomas:

"Am I going to die? I mean, that's the first thing you think."

5   With the right treatment, many women can expect to beat* the disease; but, with more than 50 drugs to choose from, it's hard for doctors to know which ones will work. Another problem is that drugs used to fight cancer are highly toxic and they kill healthy cells along with the cancerous ones. Right

10   now, choosing the right drug is a guessing game*; but it may not always be. Researchers at Vanderbilt University are using lasers to study tumor particles called organoids*.

15   Alex Walsh spoke to VOA by Skype.

—Alex Walsh, Vanderbilt University:

"Organoids are small pieces of tumor that we grow in a petri dish, and they're about 100-to-300 micrometers in

20   diameter."

They're microscopic. When given a collagen gel, the cancer cells grow as they would inside a human body. They are naturally fluorescent. So when the researchers add a cancer-fighting

25   drug, they can tell how well the drug works by measuring the amount of fluorescence.

Professor Melissa Skala is the lead researcher*.

—Melissa Skala, Vanderbilt University:

30   "Our idea was to try to eliminate toxicities from ineffective treatments and then use drugs that are more effective in treating breast cancer."

Skala spoke via Skype. She says the hope is to ultimately

beat／（病気などを）打ち負かす

guessing game／推測ゲーム

organoid／オルガノイド

lead researcher／研究主任

improve the survival of breast cancer patients.

35 —*Melissa Skala, Vanderbilt University:*

"We know a lot of breast cancer patients initially respond to their therapy and then later, their tumor starts to grow and they succumb to※ their disease."

succumb to／～で死ぬ

Skala says the next step is to see if doctors can accurately
40 predict which drugs will work in advance of the patient getting treatment. The hope is that this type of targeted therapy※ could be available to breast cancer patients in five to ten years. Then, people like Shante Thomas won't automatically think a diagnosis of breast cancer is a death sentence.

targeted therapy／標的療法（患部に限定して薬剤を送り込み、副作用を防ぐ治療法）

Read the passage and write T if the statement is true or F if it is false. Then, explain with evidence why you chose your answer.

1. Breast cancer is fatal, and Shante Thomas thought she was going to die.
　　T　F　　根拠　[..]

2. Most anticancer drugs are highly toxic and most patients don't respond to them.
　　T　F　　根拠　[..]

3. The researchers interviewed in this news used fluorescence imaging to monitor the tumors exposed to different types of anti-cancer drugs.
　　T　F　　根拠　[..]

4. Melissa Skala hopes customizing a drug for patients before chemotherapy will significantly improve the odds for successful treatment.
　　T　F　　根拠　[..]

The following is a short explanation of the targeted treatment. Read the passage again and fill in the blanks.

Experiments conducted at Vanderbilt University are vital in the fight against (¹   ). Alex Walsh is using a (²   ) to make what she calls organoids glow. Organoids are small pieces of a patient's (³   ) that are about 100-to-300 micrometers in diameter. Organoids that are grown in a petri dish are dosed with cancer drugs and placed under a microscope. The tiny tumor is then blasted with a laser. That laser light makes the organoids glow because they are naturally (⁴   ). The organoids glow to different (⁵   ) based on their response to the chemo drugs. It means that the result tells the researchers which drugs are (⁶   ) for a patient.

III CRITICAL THINKING CHALLENGE

What's your opinion about the following question?

Cancer treatment is often a painful process for patients and their families to go through.

Which is more important, the doctor's decision or the patient's wishes?

Collect information from the Internet and explain your ideas.

Step 1

Exchange ideas with your partner.

Step 2

What do you think? Explain your ideas briefly. You can use expressions from this passage, Summary, or Useful Expressions below.

Step 3

Let's make a presentation.

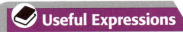 **Useful Expressions**

- The problem is that 〜（問題は〜である）

  例 The problem is that we don't have enough money.

- In my view（私の意見では）

  例 In my view, the suggested solution is inadequate.

- One of the factors might be 〜（要因の１つは〜かもしれない）

  例 One of the factors might be the difference in their learning experience.

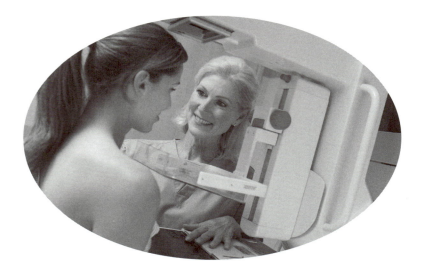

 e-Learning Exercise

1 Listening
EnglishCentral のサイトにアクセスし、News を聞きながらスクリプトの
空欄を埋めなさい。

2 Speaking
EnglishCentral のサイトにアクセスし、Speaking チェックをしなさい。

UNIT 11

Doctors Unveil Potential New Tool to Fight Brain Cancer

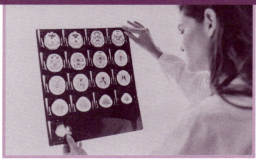

科学の世界では偶発的な大発見があります。
みなさんの身近に使うものも偶発的な発見
から生まれたものがあります。どのような
ものがあると思いますか？　本文の内容に
入る前に、ペアで意見交換してみましょう。

I VOCABULARY

CD 1-32

A. *Match each word with its definition.*

1. deliver [　　] **2.** potentially [　　]
3. opportunity [　　] **4.** experimental [　　]
5. compromised [　　]

> 選択肢
>
> ア. possibly but not yet actually
> イ. to take something to a particular place
> ウ. based on or used in scientific tests
> エ. a chance to do something when it is easy for you to do something
> オ. unable to function optimally

B. *Match each medical word with its meaning.*

1. chemotherapy [　　] **2.** ovarian [　　]
3. laser therapy [　　] **4.** probe [　　]
5. unintended effect [　　] **6.** circulation [　　]
7. peripheral system [　　] **8.** neurosurgeon [　　]

> 選択肢
>
> ア. レーザー治療　　イ. 意図していない効果　　ウ. 循環　　エ. 卵巣の
> オ. 周辺系・末梢系　　カ. 化学療法　　キ. 脳神経外科医　　ク. 探針

II COMPREHENSION

DVD CD 1-33

Step 1 **Listening Comprehension**

Watch the news and discuss the main topic with your partner.

....

....

Neurosurgeons※ have been using lasers to treat brain cancer since 2009, but now they say the technique may also allow them to deliver chemotherapy drugs directly into the brain. The key is getting past the protective blood-brain barrier※, which

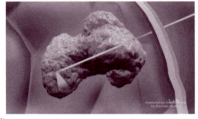

5　does its job so well it also keeps out potentially lifesaving chemotherapy drugs. Kathy Smith has ovarian cancer that spread to her brain, a type of

10　brain cancer called glioblastoma※.

—Kathy Smith, brain cancer patient:

"And there were I believe three tumors at that time and I was not at all happy about those critters."

She was treated with laser therapy. Doctors insert a tiny

15　probe into the brain, directly to the cancer where it burns up the tumor from the inside out. According to Washington University Neurosurgery※ Professor Eric Leuthardt, during the procedure it was discovered the therapy had an unintended effect on the blood-brain barrier.

20　*—Eric Leuthardt, neurosurgeon, Washington University:*

"We were basically able to show that this blood-brain barrier is broken down for around four weeks after you do this laser therapy. So not only are you killing the tumor, you are

actually opening up a window

25　of opportunity to deliver various drugs and chemicals and therapies that could otherwise not get in there."

In Kathy's case, a powerful, experimental chemotherapy

30　drug called doxorubicin※, which has been notoriously※ hard to get past the barrier was delivered directly into her brain.

—Eric Leuthardt, neurosurgeon, Washington University:

"I think what's really interesting is the blood-brain barrier

neurosurgeon／神経外科医

blood-brain barrier／血液脳関門（血液と脳の組織液との間の物質交換を制限する働きをする）

glioblastoma／膠芽腫（こうがしゅ、脳腫瘍の一種）

neurosurgery／神経外科

doxorubicin／ドキソルビシン（抗がん剤の一種）
notoriously／〜で有名な

is a two-way street, by breaking
35   it down you can get things into
the brain, but also by breaking
it down, now things can go
from your brain out into your
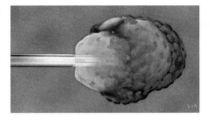
circulation, to your peripheral system, which includes your
40   immune system."

     And the immune system helps fight cancer.

     The procedure is dangerous, a compromised blood-brain
barrier puts the brain at risk, but so far it's worked well for
Smith. Patients diagnosed
45   with glioblastoma tumors
usually survive just 15
months after diagnosis.
But Smith has been
fighting her cancer since
50   2009.

—*Kathy Smith, brain cancer patient:*

     "Kind of makes you smile when they say , "Oh, you are a
good candidate for something new," and so I got worked into
that study, got worked into that, and it did work out beautifully."
55   The team of neurosurgeons from Washington University
in St. Louis are hoping to publish a more formal report on their
work later this year.

Read the passage and write T if the statement is true or F if it is false. Then, explain with evidence why you chose your answer.

1. Potentially helpful chemotherapy drugs are blocked by the blood-brain barrier.

　T　F　根拠　[....]

2. Professor Eric Leuthardt intentionally conducted laser therapy to break down a patient's blood-brain barrier.

　T　F　根拠　[....]

3. Laser therapy breaks down the blood-brain barrier but leaves it open for only a short time to effectively deliver chemotherapy drugs.

　T　F　根拠　[....]

4. Doxorubicin is a powerful unapproved chemotherapy drug that is unlikely to penetrate the blood-brain barrier.

　T　F　根拠　[....]

5. The new technique is so safe and effective that it could be a new treatment option for patients with the deadly disease.

　T　F　根拠　[....]

(**Step 3**) **Summary**　　　　　　　　　　　　　　　　🎧 1-34

The following is a short explanation of the new technique for treating glioblastoma. Read the passage again and fill in the blanks.

Glioblastoma is one form of deadly brain (¹　　　　　　　). Surgery, radiation and chemotherapy waste patients' precious time and in most cases they do not provide a cure. Now, researchers have found a high-tech laser surgery that may have an added benefit for patients. Laser surgery can open the protective blood-brain barrier, which enables (²　　　　　　　) drugs to reach brain tumors. The laser (³　　　　　　) the barrier open for about four weeks after the surgery, allowing time for drugs to (⁴　　　　　　　). Thus, the new technique might improve (⁵　　　　　　) of deadly brain cancer. The researchers said the discovery was not (⁶　　　　　　　) and they are surprised to find that the laser therapy penetrated the protective blood-brain barrier.

III CRITICAL THINKING CHALLENGE ⠿

What's your opinion about the following question?

What is the latest technology for treating brain cancer?

Collect information from the Internet and explain your ideas.

Step 1

Exchange ideas with your partner.

Step 2

What do you think? Explain your ideas briefly. You can use expressions from this passage, Summary, or Useful Expressions below.

Step 3

Let's make a presentation.

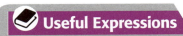 **Useful Expressions**

- Without a doubt （疑いなく）
  例 Without a doubt, his suggestion is right.

- Unfortunately, we are unable to ～ （残念ながら、私たちは～することができない）
  例 Unfortunately, we are unable to solve the problem soon.

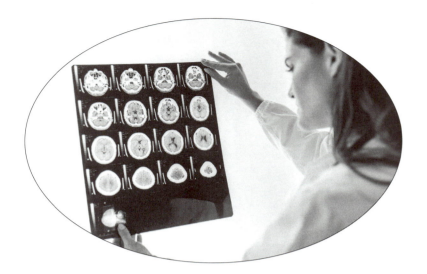

 e-Learning Exercise

1 Listening
EnglishCentral のサイトにアクセスし、News を聞きながらスクリプトの空欄を埋めなさい。

2 Speaking
EnglishCentral のサイトにアクセスし、Speaking チェックをしなさい。

Chapter 3

医療の進歩の裏側

UNIT 12

World Action Needed to Prevent Widespread Antibiotic Resistance

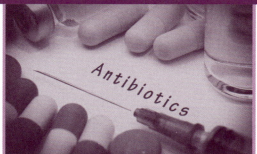

抗生物質は細菌を殺す薬です。近年は抗生物質に対して耐性を持っている細菌が表れ、抗生剤治療が効かなくなっています。耐性が生まれた原因は何だと思いますか？本文の内容に入る前に、ペアで意見交換してみましょう。

I VOCABULARY

CD 1-35

A. *Match each word with its definition.*

1. era [　　] 2. infant [　　]
3. evolve [　　] 4. generate [　　]
5. urgent [　　]

> 選択肢
> ア. to develop gradually
> イ. to produce or cause something
> ウ. a child in the first period of life
> エ. a period of time marked by distinctive character or events
> オ. requiring immediate action or attention

B. *Match each medical word with its meaning.*

1. resistance [　　] 2. drug resistance [　　]
3. germ [　　] 4. bacterial [　　]
5. prescribe [　　] 6. practitioner [　　]
7. spread [　　] 8. infection control [　　]

> 選択肢
> ア. 感染予防　　イ. 細菌性の　　ウ. 耐性　　エ. 菌
> オ. 薬物耐性　　カ. 処方する　　キ. 拡大・蔓延　　ク. 開業医・現場の人

II COMPREHENSION

DVD CD 1-36

(Step 1) Listening Comprehension

Watch the news and discuss the main topic with your partner.

....

....

73

In 2015, the World Health Organization※ warned that we are heading toward a "post-antibiotic era※," when more people will die from common infections.

—Dr. Michael Bell, Centers for Disease Control:

5 "In India alone, there is an estimated 58,000 infants who have died because of a single resistant infection in just one year."

10 The CDC estimates 23,000 people died in the US in 2014 because of drug resistance. Dr. Michael Bell says the problem is huge.

15 *—Dr. Michael Bell, Centers for Disease Control:*

"For the longest time, we've had a number of different antibiotics in the pipeline at any given time, and so whenever we ran out of the ability to use one, we would move to the next 20 one. Unfortunately, right now the number of antibiotics in the pipeline is essentially zero."

Bacteria are constantly evolving, so those that survive the drugs designed to kill them reproduce, that's normal and antibiotics themselves do not cause resistance. But improper 25 antibiotic use is one of the key drivers※ for the development of antibiotic-resistant germs. To make matters worse, most people don't understand that antibiotics can be effective only against bacterial infections, not for viruses like the flu or a cold. 30 To resolve the crisis, scientists are working on developing new drugs.

World Health Organization／世界保健機構
post-antibiotic era／抗生物質後時代

driver／原動力

74

—*Dr. Michael Bell, Centers for Disease Control:*

"But more crucially right now is saving what we have."

35   A CDC study found US hospitals were prescribing stronger drugs and more drugs than necessary. The agency asked hospital practitioners to be more careful in prescribing antibiotics. The CDC is also looking at the causes of infection.

—*Dr. Michael Bell, Centers for Disease Control:*

40   "Antibiotic resistance is not only being generated by using too many antibiotics, but also by spread of infection from lack of hygiene, from unintended contact with soiled surfaces, things of that sort so the infection control side is equally important."

    Individuals can also help. On its website, the CDC tells

45 people to take all antibiotics as prescribed and to finish the course of the drugs even if they feel better. Still, urgent action on a global level is needed to prevent the catastrophe※ that a post-antibiotic era would cause.

catastrophe／大惨事

Read the passage and write T if the statement is true or F if it is false. Then, explain with evidence why you chose your answer.

1. The post-antibiotic era refers to a time when antibiotics had not been invented.

    T   F   根拠 [....]

2. Right now we face a deficiency of antibiotic drugs to treat infectious diseases.

    T   F   根拠 [....]

3. It is commonly known that antibiotics are a range of powerful drugs that kill viruses or slow their growth.

    T   F   根拠 [....]

4. The CDC pointed out some doctors did not pay enough attention to the necessary quantity of drugs.

    T   F   根拠 [....]

5. Patients should stop taking antibiotics right after they feel better.

    T   F   根拠 [....]

The following is a short explanation of antibiotic resistance. Read the passage again and fill in the blanks.

The risk of antibiotic resistance is (1   ) to high levels in all parts of the world. It threatens our ability to treat (2   ) infectious diseases. Antibiotics are medicines used to prevent and treat (3   ) infections, but most people think antibiotics are effective in killing (4   ) such as flu or a cold. When bacteria change in response to the use of these medicines, they become antibiotic-resistant. The world urgently needs to change the way it prescribes and uses antibiotics. For example, health professionals should prescribe antibiotics when they are needed. Behavior changes including actions to reduce the (5   ) of infections through good hygiene are also important.

III CRITICAL THINKING CHALLENGE

What's your opinion about the following question?

What is an antibiotic-resistant bacterium?

Collect information from the Internet and explain it.

Step 1

Exchange ideas with your partner.

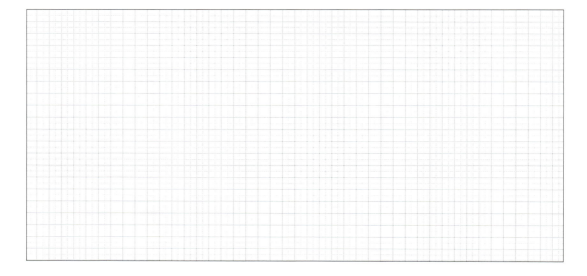

Step 2

What do you think? Explain your ideas briefly. You can use expressions from this passage, Summary, or Useful Expressions below.

Step 3

Let's make a presentation.

Useful Expressions

- It was due to 〜 （それは〜が原因だった）
  例 It was due to his mistake.

- Compared to the past 〜 （以前と比べると）
  例 Compared to the past, his skill is improving.

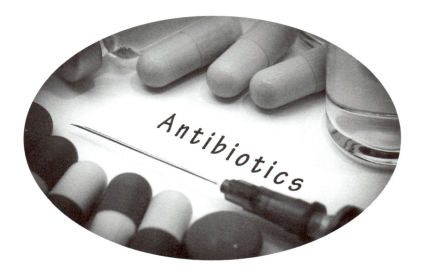

 e-Learning Exercise

1 Listening

EnglishCentral のサイトにアクセスし、News を聞きながらスクリプトの空欄を埋めなさい。

2 Speaking

EnglishCentral のサイトにアクセスし、Speaking チェックをしなさい。

Activists Push to Limit Antibiotic Use in Livestock

抗生物質は人間の病気の治療以外にも多く
使われています。それは何だと思いますか？
本文の内容に入る前に、ペアで意見交換し
てみましょう。

I VOCABULARY

CD 1-38

A. *Match each word with its definition.*

1. livestock [ ]   2. compensate for [ ]
3. willingly [ ]   4. ban [ ]
5. justify [ ]

> 選択肢
>
> ア. to give an acceptable explanation for something that other people think is
>   unreasonable
> イ. animals kept or raised for use
> ウ. readily and enthusiastically
> エ. to forbid something, especially officially
> オ. to make up

B. *Match each medical word with its meaning.*

1. overuse [ ]   2. antibiotic [ ]
3. dose [ ]   4. respond [ ]
5. antibiotic-free [ ]   6. growth promoter [ ]

> 選択肢
>
> ア. 投与量   イ. 過剰使用   ウ. 抗生物質を使っていない
> エ. 成長促進物質   オ. 抗生物質   カ. 効果を示す

II COMPREHENSION

DVD CD 1-39

(**Step** **1**) **Listening Comprehension**

Watch the news and discuss the main topic with your partner.

79

Shoppers flock to[※] the Boulder Farmers' Market[※]. Lilly Adams is here to ask them to support her petition demanding a reduction of antibiotic use in livestock.

—*Lilly Adams, Food & Water Watch:*

5　　"We are working to stop the overuse of antibiotics on factory farms. 80 percent of our antibiotics in the United States are actually used on factory

10 farms to compensate for really filthy[※], crowded conditions."

Consumer Reports indicates the majority of US shoppers worry about the daily doses of antibiotics farmers give livestock to reduce illness and speed growth.

—*Lilly Adams, Food & Water Watch:*

　　"And this isn't how antibiotics are meant to be used, so this

15 overuse of the antibiotics is causing antibiotic-resistant bacteria to grow in the farms, and this spreads into our environment."

And that leads to more infections that do not respond to available drugs. Many farmers do raise livestock without

20 antibiotics and many customers willingly pay more for antibiotic-free beef and bacon from antibiotic-free pigs.

—*Tory Hancock, Ploughshares Community Farm:*

　　"You give the animals a stress-free environment and a healthy diet, you know, really good feed, and you generally

25 don't need it."

Consumer pressure has been a major force in bringing about that change, says Anna Zorzet, a scientist and activist who spoke at the American Association for the Advancement of Science[※] annual meeting[※].

30 —*Anna Zorzet, Team ReAct Europe:*

　　"Sweden was the first country in the world to ban the use of antibiotics as growth promoters in 1986, and the EU followed suit in 2006. The farmers felt that they couldn't justify the use of

flock to／～に押し寄せる
farmers' market／農産物の直売市

filthy／不潔な

American Association for the Advancement of Science／アメリカ科学振興協会
annual meeting／年次会合

antibiotics, and the public opinion was quite a lot against it."

35 US consumers are moving in this direction as well. According to the National Farm Foundation, an educational nonprofit group※, which is holding seminars nationwide to prepare farmers for stricter government rules on antibiotics. Foundation President Neil Conklin says that many companies

40 are already planning to eliminate regular load doses of these medicines.

—Neil Conklin, National Farm Foundation:

"Chick-fil-A※ and McDonald's, there are companies like Tyson※ and Perdue※ that

45 are making big changes in the way they are running their production systems in response to this consumer demand."

And the activism continues.

50 *—Activist:*

"We're asking college students to tell Subway that they want them to stop selling meat raised with antibiotics."

Late last month, Subway announced that it would begin to phase out antibiotic use in its meat in its US stores. Activists

55 hope reduced antibiotic use will mean medicines across the globe have a better chance of fighting infections.

nonprofit group／非営利団体

Chick-fil-A／チックフィレイ（鶏肉料理に特化したアメリカ大手レストラン・チェーン）
Tyson／タイソンフーズ（アメリカの食品メーカー）
Perdue／パーデューファームズ（アメリカの鶏肉処理会社）

Read the passage and write T if the statement is true or F if it is false. Then, explain with evidence why you chose your answer.

1. Although most antibiotics are used for treating human diseases, factory farmers also administer them to their animals.

☐ T ☐ F ■根拠 [..]

2. Lilly Adams claims that the use of antibiotics in animal feed for disease prevention and growth promotion is inappropriate.

☐ T ☐ F ■根拠 [..]

3. Overusing antibiotics for livestock is a threat to human health.

☐ T ☐ F ■根拠 [..]

4. Customers are reluctant to spend more money on meat from animals that have not received antibiotics.

☐ T ☐ F ■根拠 [..]

5. The US government is expected to regulate the use of antibiotics in livestock to solve the growing problem of antibiotic resistance.

☐ T ☐ F ■根拠 [..]

(Step 3) Summary

CD 1-40

The following is a short explanation of antibiotic overuse in animals. Read the passage again and fill in the blanks.

Antibiotics must be used responsibly not only in humans but also in (^{1}). (^{2}) of antibiotics causes the development and (^{3}) of antibiotic-resistant bacteria. Inappropriate antibiotic use such as growth promotion in livestock may lead to the survival and growth of resistant bacteria. First, Sweden introduced a (^{4}) in 1986. Then other countries in the EU (^{5}) in 2006. The EU decided to stop using antibiotics to promote growth in food animals. In the US, big food companies like Tyson and Perdue and fast-food chains like Chick-fil-A and McDonald's are trying to respond to such (^{6}) from customers. Subway also announced that it would not use meat that comes from animals given antibiotics.

Ⅲ CRITICAL THINKING CHALLENGE

What's your opinion about the following question?

Should we use antibiotics for agriculture or not?

Collect information from the Internet and explain your ideas.

Step 1

Exchange ideas with your partner.

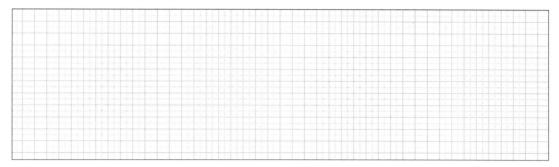

Step 2

What do you think? Explain your ideas briefly. You can use expressions from this passage, Summary, or Useful Expressions below.

Step 3

Let's make a presentation.

 Useful Expressions

- The major obstacle is 〜 （重大な障害は〜である）

  例 The major obstacle is a cultural difference between them.

- In my opinion, we should 〜 （私の意見では〜すべきである）

  例 In my opinion, we should solve the problem very quickly.

- The next step is to deal with 〜 （次のステップは〜に取り組むことである）

  例 The next step is to deal with your fear of failure.

 e-Learning Exercise

1 Listening

EnglishCentral のサイトにアクセスし、News を聞きながらスクリプトの空欄を埋めなさい。

2 Speaking

EnglishCentral のサイトにアクセスし、Speaking チェックをしなさい。

Oregon Case Renews Right-to-Die Debate

もし自分が不治の病で余命が半年と分かれば、どのように過ごしますか？ 本文の内容に入る前に、ペアで意見交換してみましょう。

I VOCABULARY

CD 1-41

A. *Match each word with its definition.*

1. severe   [   ]   **2.** launch   [   ]
3. opposition   [   ]   **4.** generally   [   ]
5. abuse   [   ]

> 選択肢
>
> ア. very painful or harmful
> イ. usually or most of the time
> ウ. to start something, usually big or important
> エ. the use of something in a way that it should not be used
> オ. strong disagreement with something

B. *Match each medical word with its meaning.*

1. headache   [   ]   **2.** aggressive form of   [   ]
3. incurable   [   ]   **4.** unbearable   [   ]
5. terminal   [   ]   **6.** life-ending medication   [   ]
7. ethical standard   [   ]   **8.** implement   [   ]

> 選択肢
>
> ア. 不治の   イ. 末期の   ウ. 致死薬   エ. 実行する
> オ. 頭痛   カ. 耐えられない   キ. 倫理基準   ク. 攻撃的な～の形態・侵襲性の強い

II COMPREHENSION

DVD CD 1-42

Step 1 **Listening Comprehension**

Watch the news and discuss the main topic with your partner.

....

....

Brittany Maynard was a vibrant[*] young newlywed when she started to suffer from severe headaches.

—*Brittany Maynard:*

5 "I didn't understand them because I had never had anything like that before in my life."

Doctors told Maynard she had an aggressive form of brain cancer and had just six months to live.

10 —*Brittany Maynard:*

"Right when I was diagnosed, my husband and I were actively trying for a family, which is heartbreaking for us both."

Aware that her cancer was incurable, Maynard decided she'd rather die on her own terms[*] than go through unbearable

15 pain and suffering. So she and her family moved from California to Oregon, where the state's Death with Dignity Act[*] allows people with a terminal illness to get life-ending medication from

20 their doctor so they can die peacefully.

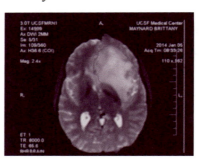

—*Brittany Maynard:*

"I can't even tell you the amount of relief that it provides me to know that I don't have to die the way that it's been

25 described to me that my brain tumor would take me on its own."

Maynard chose to end her life on November 1st.

—*Brittany Maynard:*

"I will die upstairs in my bedroom that I share with my husband, with my mother and my husband by my side."

30 During her remaining time, she launched a campaign to raise awareness about the importance of choice in the right-to-die[*] debate. And she spent time with her loved ones before she took a lethal amount of drugs and died as she had wished.

vibrant／活発な

on one's own terms／自分の思うように

Death with Dignity Act／尊厳死法

right-to-die／死ぬ権利

Her decision was supported by George Eighmey, a board
35 member of the Death with Dignity National Center. But he told
VOA via Skype that not everyone would agree with her choice.

—George Eighmey, Death with Dignity National Center:

"The main opposition is religious, and so when it's a
religious opposition, all I can say is: I respect your beliefs, I
40 respect you, please respect our option to use this law. The other
opposition is generally from either physicians who believe that
they shouldn't be doing this because of their ethical standards,
or they believe that there may be abuses. Well, we have set up
all these safeguards※ to prevent the abuses."

safeguard／予防対策

45 The right-to-die issue is still an open question, said Cynda
Rushton, a professor at Johns Hopkins' Berman Institute of
Bioethics and School of Nursing.

—Cynda Rushton, Johns Hopkins' Berman Institute of Bioethics
and School of Nursing:

50 "Having a policy that allows people to have choices at the
end of life does not then mean that everyone has to follow that
particular path. What we've learned in Oregon is that having a
law has allowed people to request this process to be initiated,
but actually a small number have ended up implementing that
55 request."

But Brittany Maynard who did make that request gave
some advice about living before she died.

—Brittany Maynard:

"Seize the day. What's important to you? What do you care
60 about? What matters? Pursue that. Forget the rest."

Read the passage and write T if the statement is true or F if it is false. Then, explain with evidence why you chose your answer.

1. Brittany Maynard chose to have life-ending medication because she did not want to experience unnecessary suffering at the end of her life.

   ☐ T ☐ F   根拠 [....]

2. Brittany Maynard moved to Oregon because there was no treatment that would save her life in the hospital in California.

   ☐ T ☐ F   根拠 [....]

3. Only Brittany Maynard's husband and her mother fully supported her decision on assisted suicide.

   ☐ T ☐ F   根拠 [....]

4. Religion, ethical issues and worry about abuses are the main source of opposition to contemporary end-of-life-care debates.

   ☐ T ☐ F   根拠 [....]

5. The safeguards provided by Death with Dignity National Center will end an intensifying debate concerning end-of-life options for terminally ill patients.

   ☐ T ☐ F   根拠 [....]

(Step 3) Summary

🎧 1-43

The following is a short explanation of Brittany Maynard's life. Read the passage again and fill in the blanks.

Brittany Maynard, a terminally ill 29-year-old, decided to take lethal drugs prescribed by her physician. When she was ([1]   ) with brain cancer, the doctor told her that she had six months to live. Then she made her decision: doctor-assisted ([2]   ). In an interview, she described the severity of her physical and emotional ([3]   ) as well as the ([4]   ) of knowing she could end her dying process peacefully with her family. After her decision, Brittany and her husband ([5]   ) to Oregon to gain access to the state's Death with Dignity Act. She spent her final days conducting a campaign to ([6]   ) awareness about Death with Dignity Act. The right-to-die issue is still being debated.

III CRITICAL THINKING CHALLENGE

What's your opinion about the following question?

Do we have the right to die or not?

Collect information from the Internet and explain your ideas.

Step 1

Exchange ideas with your partner.

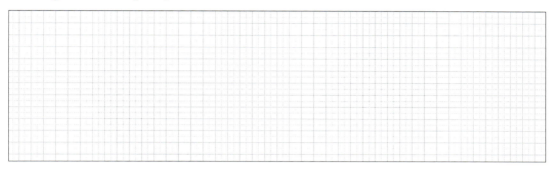

Step 2

What do you think? Explain your ideas briefly. You can use expressions from this passage, Summary, or Useful Expressions below.

Step 3

Let's make a presentation.

 **Useful Expressions**

- I'm for the idea of 〜（私は〜という考えに賛成である）
  例 I'm for the idea of banning the use of the chemical.

- I'm against the idea of 〜（私は〜という考えに反対である）
  例 I'm against the idea of using the chemical.

- To summarize that point（その点を要約すると）
  例 To summarize that point, losing weight is not easy.

 e-Learning Exercise

1 Listening

EnglishCentral のサイトにアクセスし、News を聞きながらスクリプトの
空欄を埋めなさい。

2 Speaking

EnglishCentral のサイトにアクセスし、Speaking チェックをしなさい。

Hospice Teams Help Patients Face Death

今日の内容はホスピスです。みなさんはホスピスという言葉は聞いたことがあるでしょう。では、ホスピスとはどのようなものでしょうか？ 本文の内容に入る前に、ペアで情報交換をしてみましょう。

I VOCABULARY

CD 1-44

A. *Match each word with its definition.*

    1. encompass   [   ]   **2.** compassion   [   ]

    3. dignity   [   ]   **4.** appreciate   [   ]

    5. embrace   [   ]

> 選択肢
>
> ア. to eagerly accept someone
> イ. to thank someone
> ウ. the fact of being respected or deserving respect
> エ. a strong feeling of sympathy for someone who is suffering and a desire to help them
> オ. to include a wide range of ideas and subjects

B. *Match each medical word with its meaning.*

    1. aggressive treatment   [   ]   **2.** radiation   [   ]

    3. scan   [   ]   **4.** hospice   [   ]

    5. hearing   [   ]   **6.** terminally   [   ]

    7. quality of life   [   ]

> 選択肢
>
> ア. スキャン   イ. ホスピス   ウ. 生活の質   エ. 末期的に
> オ. 積極的治療   カ. 聴力   キ. 放射線

II COMPREHENSION

DVD CD 1-45

(Step 1) **Listening Comprehension**

Watch the news and discuss the main topic with your partner.

Faye and Wayne Payne lived a rich and interesting life before settling down in this picturesque※ area of rural Virginia. But their peaceful existence was shattered when they learned that Faye had lung cancer. The 70-year-old retired secretary
5 endured a series of aggressive treatments that left her weak and underweight.

—Faye Payne, hospice patient:

"I did the radiation, and I did the chemo and after I had
10 the last scan done they realized I had more cancer coming up here. And I said 'No more.'"

Faye Payne
HOSPICE PATIENT

Instead, encouraged by her doctors and after talking it over with her family, Faye decided to receive hospice care. Social
15 worker Robin Johnson is part of the hospice team that visits Faye in her home.

—Robin Johnson. Hospice of the Rapidan:

"The nurse is looking at all the medical things and the social workers looking at the psycho-social spiritual things,
20 which of course can encompass a lot."

—Wayne Payne, husband of hospice patient:

"They helped me realize that, yes, death is coming, and they've helped me get ready. I now have everything lined up※ and ready to go."

25 Hospice care helps the whole family.

—Wayne Payne, husband of hospice patient:

"They come along and they take her blood pressure and check her hearing and get her medication, and it's made life a whole lot easier for both of us."

30 Melissa Mills is assistant director of patient services at Hospice of the Rapidan, which serves terminally ill patients in several counties in the state of Virginia.

—Melissa Mills, Hospice of the Rapidan:

picturesque／絵のように
美しい

line up／準備する

"We're all here for the same mission and that's to help our
35 patients die with compassion and dignity."

74-year-old Jim Sykes appreciates that philosophy.
Diagnosed two years ago with head and neck cancer, he's been
receiving hospice care at home for seven months.

—Jim Sykes, hospice patient:
40 "I would advise anybody that needs help like this, ask their
support, the hospice for what they do."

Lisa Stone is Jim's social worker.

—Lisa Stone, Hospice of the Rapidan:

"In a lot of my visits are
45 providing a lot of support of
listening. Jim has his black
book of photos so we do, what I
like to call photo-therapy."

Eric Lindner has been a hospice volunteer since 2009, and
50 has written about his experiences. He believes hospice provides
a support system that's largely missing in American culture.

—Eric Lindner, hospice volunteer:

"I've travelled a fair bit—China, Africa, other places—and
the elders are embraced and taken into the family. And in this
55 country, just the way it's developed, maybe that's the role that
hospice has tried to fill a little bit."

That support has helped patients like Faye Payne focus on
the quality of life they're enjoying today. And she says when the
time comes for her to leave this earth, she is ready.

60 *—Faye Payne, hospice patient:*

"I was born July 16, in 1942, but my dad was working on
the railroad and he died April 16, 1942, so I want to get to see
my dad one day, that's the main thing, and I'm not afraid."

Read the passage and write T if the statement is true or F if it is false. Then, explain with evidence why you chose your answer.

1. Faye Payne noticed that she had lung cancer when she experienced a decline in physical strength as well as abnormal weight loss.

T F 根拠 [....]

2. A chemotherapy and radiation therapy combination achieved an effective treatment outcome for Faye Payne.

T F 根拠 [....]

3. Faye Payne decided to stop aggressive treatments in spite of opposition by her doctor.

T F 根拠 [....]

4. Hospice care helps patients in the last phases of an incurable disease but it does not ensure that their families will receive support.

T F 根拠 [....]

5. Thanks to the support of the hospice care team, Faye Payne is ready to face death.

T F 根拠 [....]

(**Step 3**) **Summary**   1-46

The following is a short explanation of the role of hospice care. Read the passage again and fill in the blanks.

For many (¹ _____) ill patients, hospice care offers a more dignified and comfortable alternative to spending their final months in a hospital. Hospice care focuses on patients' (² _____) of life so that they can (³ _____) their remaining time with their family and friends. Hospice care is usually provided by a care team comprising a wide variety of medical professions such as doctors, (⁴ _____), social workers, and trained volunteers. For Faye Payne, the nurse provides medical support and the social worker offers psycho-social and (⁵ _____) support. Eric Lindner believes hospice care is a (⁶ _____) support system in American culture.

III CRITICAL THINKING CHALLENGE

What's your opinion about the following question?

What is the role of health care workers in hospice or terminal care?

Collect information from the Internet and explain it.

Exchange ideas with your partner.

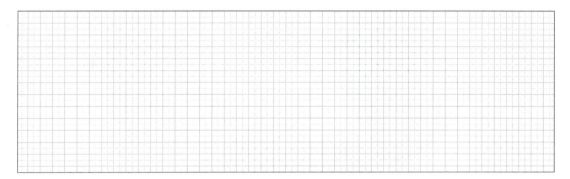

Step 2

What do you think? Explain your ideas briefly. You can use expressions from this passage, Summary, or Useful Expressions below.

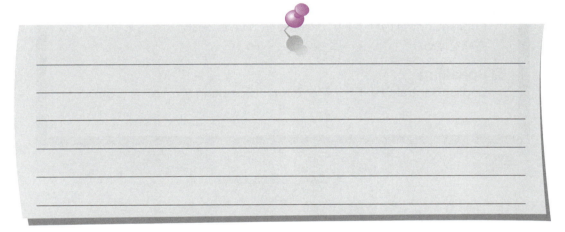

Step 3

Let's make a presentation.

- be in charge of ～（～の責任者である）
  例 The government is in charge of managing the country

- The underlying issue here is that ～（ここで根本的な問題は～である）
  例 The underlying issue here is that nobody cares about the problem.

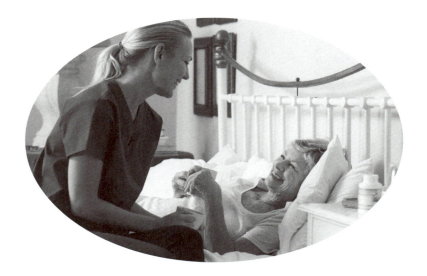

 e-Learning Exercise

1 Listening
EnglishCentral のサイトにアクセスし、News を聞きながらスクリプトの
空欄を埋めなさい。

2 Speaking
EnglishCentral のサイトにアクセスし、Speaking チェックをしなさい。

Extra Activity
1–5

Extra Activity 1

Ⅰ PREPARATION

グループに分かれプレゼンテーションの準備をしよう。

1 Unit 1 〜 4 の中から各自が作成した意見や情報（CRITICAL THINKING）をグループで見せ合い、発表するテーマを決めなさい。

....

....

2 選んだ Unit の大意とそれを踏まえて意見をグループでまとめなさい。

....

....

....

3 以下の点に注意して、発表用の台本を英語で作ろう。
1. 選んだ Unit の大意とそれを踏まえた意見を述べなさい。
2.「疑問点」や「反対意見」から発表する場合、その根拠を示しなさい。

....

....

....

....

....

....

....

....

....

4 以下の点に注意して、発表する内容を Power Point 等のプレゼンツールで作成しよう。
1. 自分たちの意見を裏付ける具体的なデータや研究成果を提示しよう。
2. インターネットの情報は、厚生労働省や WHO などの公的機関や大学などの信頼性の高いサイトから引用しましょう。

Ⅱ PRESENTATION

発表してみましょう。またあなたが聞き手の時、発表の performance を採点しよう。
採点は、*DELIVERY*（発表者の様子）と *CONTENT*（内容）の２種類で、採点は巻末の評価シートを使いなさい。

DELIVERY（発表者の様子）：Facing the audience（顔が聞き手の方を向き目線が下を向いていなかったか）、Voice（大きい声、聴きやすいスピード、強弱をつけた発音）、Posture（姿勢、立ち位置）の３つの観点

CONTENT（内容）：Visual aids（わかりやすい図・表、多すぎない文字数）と Interesting or important information（聞いて「なるほど」と思える考えがあったか）、Evidence（説得力のあるデータなどの裏付け）の３つの観点。

Useful Expressions

○**プレゼンテーションの導入：聴衆への質問・確認**
- Do you know ～？ 「～をご存じですか？」
- Have you ever heard about ～？「～についてお聞きになったことはありませんか？」
- Do you know anything about ～？「～について何かご存知でしょうか？」
※⇒ここから本論（Body）へ入る。

○**スピーチ全体の構成**

1. 話し始める
- Today, I would like to talk to you about ～「今日は～についてお話ししたいと思います」
- I chose this topic because ～「私がこの話題を選んだ理由は～」
- In this talk, I will touch on three points.「今回私が話したいのは次の３つの点です。」

2. 本論 (Body) を展開する。
- First, I will tell you about ～「最初にお話ししたいのは～」
- Second, I will talk about ～「次にお話ししたいのは～」
- Third, I will make several proposals that I think could help to solve these problems.
  「3番目に、これらの問題を解決するのに役立ついくつかの提案をしたいと思います。」

3. 最後に （聴き手からの質問やコメントを求める、質疑へ）
- Thank you for listening. Now I would like to respond to your questions or comments.
  「ご静聴ありがとうございました。さて、皆様からの質問やコメントに答えたいと思います。」

Extra Activity 2

グループに分かれプレゼンテーションの準備をしよう。

1 Unit 5 〜 7 の中から各自が作成した意見や情報（CRITICAL THINKING）をグループで見せ合い、発表するテーマを決めなさい。

....

....

2 選んだ Unit の大意とそれを踏まえて意見をグループでまとめなさい。

....

....

....

3 以下の点に注意して、発表用の台本を英語で作ろう。
1. 選んだ Unit の大意とそれを踏まえた意見を述べなさい。
2.「疑問点」や「反対意見」から発表する場合、その根拠を示しなさい。

....

....

....

....

....

....

....

....

....

....

4 以下の点に注意して、発表する内容を Power Point 等のプレゼンツールで作成しよう。
1. 自分たちの意見を裏付ける具体的なデータや研究成果を提示しよう。
2. インターネットの情報は、厚生労働省や WHO などの公的機関や大学などの信頼性の高いサイトから引用しましょう。

発表してみましょう。またあなたが聞き手の時、発表の performance を採点しよう。
採点は、*DELIVERY*（発表者の様子）と *CONTENT*（内容）の２種類で、採点は巻末の評価シート
を使いなさい。

DELIVERY（発表者の様子）：Facing the audience（顔が聞き手の方を向き目線が下を向いて
いなかったか）、Voice（大きい声、聴きやすいスピード、強弱をつけた発音）、Posture（姿勢、
立ち位置）の３つの観点

CONTENT（内容）：Visual aids（わかりやすい図・表、多すぎない文字数）と Interesting or
important information（聞いて「なるほど」と思える考えがあったか）、Evidence（説得力の
あるデータなどの裏付け）の３つの観点。

Useful Expressions

○**本論（Body）の導入：トピックの紹介やトピック選択の理由を提示する**
  • The reason why I chose this topic is that 〜「この話題を選んだ理由は〜」

○**本論（Body）の議論（Argument）：主題を提示する**
  • I would like to give you my reasons.「私なりの理由をあげてみます。」

○**本論（Body）の議論（Argument）：反対理由を提示する**
  • There are (three) reasons why I disagree.「私が反対であるのには（３つの）理由があります。」
  • I have (three) reasons why I think so.「私がそう考えるには（３つの）理由があります。」

○**本論（Body）の議論（Argument）：意見や事実を順番に述べる**
  first「まず第１に」、at first「最初に」、first of all「まず最初に」、to begin with「はじめに」
  in the end「終わりに」、finally「最後に」、lastly「最後に」

○**本論（Body）の議論（Argument）：材料や資料を追加する**
  moreover「さらに」、besides「その上に」、in addition「加えて」、furthermore「さらに」

○**本論（Body）の議論（Argument）：比較する**
  in comparison「比較すれば・それと比較して」、in comparison to 〜「〜と比較して」
  in contrast「対照的に」、compared to 〜「〜に比較すれば」

Extra Activity 3

グループに分かれプレゼンテーションの準備をしよう。

1 Unit 8 〜 11 の中から各自が作成した意見や情報（CRITICAL THINKING）をグループで見せ合い、発表するテーマを決めなさい。

....

....

2 選んだ Unit の大意とそれを踏まえて意見をグループでまとめなさい。

....

....

....

3 以下の点に注意して、発表用の台本を英語で作ろう。
1. 選んだ Unit の大意とそれを踏まえた意見を述べなさい。
2.「疑問点」や「反対意見」から発表する場合、その根拠を示しなさい。

....

....

....

....

....

....

....

....

....

4 以下の点に注意して、発表する内容を Power Point 等のプレゼンツールで作成しよう。
1. 自分たちの意見を裏付ける具体的なデータや研究成果を提示しよう。
2. インターネットの情報は、厚生労働省や WHO などの公的機関や大学などの信頼性の高いサイトから引用しましょう。

発表してみましょう。またあなたが聞き手の時、発表の performance を採点しよう。
採点は、*DELIVERY*（発表者の様子）と *CONTENT*（内容）の２種類で、採点は巻末の評価シートを使いなさい。

DELIVERY（発表者の様子）：Facing the audience（顔が聞き手の方を向き目線が下を向いていなかったか）、Voice（大きい声、聴きやすいスピード、強弱をつけた発音）、Posture（姿勢、立ち位置）の３つの観点

CONTENT（内容）：Visual aids（わかりやすい図・表、多すぎない文字数）と Interesting or important information（聞いて「なるほど」と思える考えがあったか）、Evidence（説得力のあるデータなどの裏付け）の３つの観点。

Useful Expressions

○**類似点を挙げる**

similarly「同様に（類似したものとして）」、in the same way「同じように」
likewise「同じように」

○**反論・反対・逆説（☞これまでと真逆や対照的な内容に入る標識として使えます）**

on the other hand「他方で」、on the contrary「対照的に」
however「しかしながら」、nevertheless「しかしながら」

○**話題を変える・追加する**

incidentally「付随的に、ちなみに」、by the way「ところで」

○**因果関係を示す（☞主題の結論につながるので重要）**

for this reason「この理由のために」、that is why「こういうわけで」

○**結果・結論**

- In concluding, I should note that ～「結論として～と述べておきたい。」
- Finally, it seems appropriate to remark that ～
  「最後に、～ということを指摘しておくことが妥当だ。」

Extra Activity 4

グループに分かれプレゼンテーションの準備をしよう。

1 Unit 12、13 の中から各自が作成した意見や情報（CRITICAL THINKING）をグループで見せ合い、発表するテーマを決めなさい。

....

....

2 選んだ Unit の大意とそれを踏まえて意見をグループでまとめなさい。

....

....

....

3 以下の点に注意して、発表用の台本を英語で作ろう。
1. 選んだ Unit の大意とそれを踏まえた意見を述べなさい。
2.「疑問点」や「反対意見」から発表する場合、その根拠を示しなさい。

....

....

....

....

....

....

....

....

....

4 以下の点に注意して、発表する内容を Power Point 等のプレゼンツールで作成しよう。
1. 自分たちの意見を裏付ける具体的なデータや研究成果を提示しよう。
2. インターネットの情報は、厚生労働省や WHO などの公的機関や大学などの信頼性の高いサイトから引用しましょう。

Ⅱ PRESENTATION

発表してみましょう。またあなたが聞き手の時、発表の performance を採点しよう。
採点は、*DELIVERY*（発表者の様子）と *CONTENT*（内容）の２種類で、採点は巻末の評価シートを使いなさい。

DELIVERY（発表者の様子）：Facing the audience（顔が聞き手の方を向き目線が下を向いていなかったか）、Voice（大きい声、聴きやすいスピード、強弱をつけた発音）、Posture（姿勢、立ち位置）の３つの観点

CONTENT（内容）：Visual aids（わかりやすい図・表、多すぎない文字数）と Interesting or important information（聞いて「なるほど」と思える考えがあったか）、Evidence（説得力のあるデータなどの裏付け）の３つの観点。

Useful Expressions

○質疑：質問をする前の表現
- Thank you for your presentation. I was especially happy to hear that 〜 .
  Now I have a question to ask.
  「ご発表ありがとうございました。〜をうかがい、特にうれしく思いました。
  さて質問があります。」

○質疑：質問をする
- If I may ask a question, what do you mean by 〜 ?
  「〜がどういう意味なのか、お伺いしたいのですが？」
- If I may ask a question, what do you mean by that statement?
  「そのお話しがどういう意味なのか、お伺いしたいのですが？」
- Would you clarify your last point?「最後の１点を説明していただけますか？」

○質疑：質問に答える
- This is an extremely (= very) difficult question to answer.
  「お答えするのに非常に難しい質問です。」
  ※質問に対し、まず第一声で使える表現（時間稼ぎ）
- As for your (first) question, I should say that 〜
  「あなたの（第１の）質問について、私は〜と言いたい」

○質疑：質問を聞き返す
- Would you please repeat the question?「もう一度ご質問をお願いします。」
- I would like to have your (second) question repeated? I didn't really understand it.
  「あなたの（２番目の）質問を繰り返していただけませんか？　よくわかりませんでした。」

  ※質問された人は、質問がわからなければはっきり聞き返しましょう。
  ※発表者が聞き返した場合は、質問者は必ず質問をわかりやすく「言い換え」ましょう。つまり、
  　同じ質問表現を繰り返さないようにしましょう。

Ⅰ PREPARATION

グループに分かれプレゼンテーションの準備をしよう。

1 Unit 14、15 の中から各自が作成した意見や情報（CRITICAL THINKING）をグループで見せ合い、発表するテーマを決めなさい。

....

....

2 選んだ Unit の大意とそれを踏まえて意見をグループでまとめなさい。

....

....

....

3 以下の点に注意して、発表用の台本を英語で作ろう。
  1. 選んだ Unit の大意とそれを踏まえた意見を述べなさい。
  2.「疑問点」や「反対意見」から発表する場合、その根拠を示しなさい。

....

....

....

....

....

....

....

....

....

4 以下の点に注意して、発表する内容を Power Point 等のプレゼンツールで作成しよう。
  1. 自分たちの意見を裏付ける具体的なデータや研究成果を提示しよう。
  2. インターネットの情報は、厚生労働省や WHO などの公的機関や大学などの信頼性の高いサイトから引用しましょう。

Ⅱ PRESENTATION ::::

発表してみましょう。またあなたが聞き手の時、発表の performance を採点しよう。
採点は、*DELIVERY*（発表者の様子）と *CONTENT*（内容）の２種類で、採点は巻末の評価シート
を使いなさい。

DELIVERY（発表者の様子）：Facing the audience（顔が聞き手の方を向き目線が下を向いて
いなかったか）、Voice（大きい声、聴きやすいスピード、強弱をつけた発音）、Posture（姿勢、
立ち位置）の３つの観点

CONTENT（内容）：Visual aids（わかりやすい図・表、多すぎない文字数）と Interesting or
important information（聞いて「なるほど」と思える考えがあったか）、Evidence（説得力の
あるデータなどの裏付け）の３つの観点。

Useful Expressions

○質疑：総括的な質問をする
- All in all, what was the result of your presentation?
  「結局、今回のご発表にはどういう成果があったのでしょうか？」
- What do you think are the best procedures for solving the problem?
  「問題の解決には、どのような方法が最善とお考えですか？」

○質疑：その他の表現
- What procedures (ways) do you recommend?
  「どのような方法がよいと思いますか？」
- Have you made any comparison of your conclusion with ～ yet?
  「あなたの結論と～とを比較なさっていますか？」
- How do your results compare with the theory?
  「結果を理論と比べると、どうなりますか？」
- In the end, are the results consistent with the theory?
  「結果は理論と一致しましたか？」

プレゼンテーション後の質疑の意味
※発表の目的は（問題解決学習の場合）問題解決を全員で探すことです。
※発表後の質疑が、発表者のあら捜し（finding his/her fault）ではいけません。

TEXT PRODUCTION STAFF

edited by Mitsugu Shishido	編集 宍戸 貢
English-language editing by Bill Benfield	英文校閲 ビル・ベンフィールド
cover design by SEIN	表紙デザイン ザイン

CD PRODUCTION STAFF

recorded by	吹き込み者
Howard Colefield (AmE)	ハワード・コールフィールド（アメリカ英語）
Edith Kayumi (AmE)	イーディス・カユミ（アメリカ英語）
Jack Merluzzi (AmE)	ジャック・マルージー（アメリカ英語）
Vinay Murthy (AmE)	ヴィナイ・マーシー（アメリカ英語）

Medical Front Line
VOAで深める医療の世界

2019年 1 月10日　初版　発行
2025年 3 月 5 日　第 7 刷 発行

編著者　　眞砂 薫　　田中 博晃　　Bill Benfield
発行者　　佐野 英一郎
発行所　　株式会社 成美堂
　　　　　〒101-0052　東京都千代田区神田小川町3-22
　　　　　TEL 03-3291-2261　FAX 03-3293-5490
　　　　　https://www.seibido.co.jp

印刷・製本　　(株)加藤文明社

ISBN 978-4-7919-7192-3　　　　　　　　　　　Printed in Japan

- ✂ 切り取り ✂ -

Date (　　　/　　　)　PRESENTATION GROUP (No.　　)　得点　　/10

DELIVERY（発表者の様子）　**Weak**　　　　**Average**　　　　**Great**

1　　2　　3　　4　　5

Comment: (　　　　　　　　　　　　　　　　　　　　　　　　　　　　　)

CONTENT（内容）　1　　2　　3　　4　　5

Comment: (　　　　　　　　　　　　　　　　　　　　　　　　　　　　　)

- ✂ 切り取り ✂ -

Date (　　　/　　　)　PRESENTATION GROUP (No.　　)　得点　　/10

DELIVERY（発表者の様子）　**Weak**　　　　**Average**　　　　**Great**

1　　2　　3　　4　　5

Comment: (　　　　　　　　　　　　　　　　　　　　　　　　　　　　　)

CONTENT（内容）　1　　2　　3　　4　　5

Comment: (　　　　　　　　　　　　　　　　　　　　　　　　　　　　　)

- ✂ 切り取り ✂ -

Date (　　　/　　　)　PRESENTATION GROUP (No.　　)　得点　　/10

DELIVERY（発表者の様子）　**Weak**　　　　**Average**　　　　**Great**

1　　2　　3　　4　　5

Comment: (　　　　　　　　　　　　　　　　　　　　　　　　　　　　　)

CONTENT（内容）　1　　2　　3　　4　　5

Comment: (　　　　　　　　　　　　　　　　　　　　　　　　　　　　　)

- ✂ 切り取り ✂ -

Date (　　　/　　　)　PRESENTATION GROUP (No.　　)　得点　　/10

DELIVERY（発表者の様子）　**Weak**　　　　**Average**　　　　**Great**

1　　2　　3　　4　　5

Comment: (　　　　　　　　　　　　　　　　　　　　　　　　　　　　　)

CONTENT（内容）　1　　2　　3　　4　　5

Comment: (　　　　　　　　　　　　　　　　　　　　　　　　　　　　　)

- ✂ 切り取り ✂ -

Date (　　　/　　　)　PRESENTATION GROUP (No.　　)　得点　　/10

DELIVERY（発表者の様子）　**Weak**　　　　**Average**　　　　**Great**

1　　2　　3　　4　　5

Comment: (　　　　　　　　　　　　　　　　　　　　　　　　　　　　　)

CONTENT（内容）　1　　2　　3　　4　　5

Comment: (　　　　　　　　　　　　　　　　　　　　　　　　　　　　　)

- ✂ 切り取り ✂ -

Date (　　　/　　　)　PRESENTATION GROUP (No.　　)　得点　　/10

DELIVERY（発表者の様子）　**Weak**　　　　**Average**　　　　**Great**

1　　2　　3　　4　　5

Comment: (　　　　　　　　　　　　　　　　　　　　　　　　　　　　　)

CONTENT（内容）　1　　2　　3　　4　　5

Comment: (　　　　　　　　　　　　　　　　　　　　　　　　　　　　　)

- ✂ 切り取り ✂ -

name :

name :

name :

name :

name :

name :

------ ✄ 切り取り ✄ ------

Date (　　　/　　　) PRESENTATION GROUP (No.　　) 得点　　　/10

DELIVERY（発表者の様子）　**Weak**　　　　**Average**　　　　**Great**

　　　　　　　　　　　　　1　　　2　　　3　　　4　　　5

Comment: (　　　　　　　　　　　　　　　　　　　　　)

CONTENT（内容）　　　　1　　　2　　　3　　　4　　　5

Comment: (　　　　　　　　　　　　　　　　　　　　　)

------ ✄ 切り取り ✄ ------

Date (　　　/　　　) PRESENTATION GROUP (No.　　) 得点　　　/10

DELIVERY（発表者の様子）　**Weak**　　　　**Average**　　　　**Great**

　　　　　　　　　　　　　1　　　2　　　3　　　4　　　5

Comment: (　　　　　　　　　　　　　　　　　　　　　)

CONTENT（内容）　　　　1　　　2　　　3　　　4　　　5

Comment: (　　　　　　　　　　　　　　　　　　　　　)

------ ✄ 切り取り ✄ ------

Date (　　　/　　　) PRESENTATION GROUP (No.　　) 得点　　　/10

DELIVERY（発表者の様子）　**Weak**　　　　**Average**　　　　**Great**

　　　　　　　　　　　　　1　　　2　　　3　　　4　　　5

Comment: (　　　　　　　　　　　　　　　　　　　　　)

CONTENT（内容）　　　　1　　　2　　　3　　　4　　　5

Comment: (　　　　　　　　　　　　　　　　　　　　　)

------ ✄ 切り取り ✄ ------

Date (　　　/　　　) PRESENTATION GROUP (No.　　) 得点　　　/10

DELIVERY（発表者の様子）　**Weak**　　　　**Average**　　　　**Great**

　　　　　　　　　　　　　1　　　2　　　3　　　4　　　5

Comment: (　　　　　　　　　　　　　　　　　　　　　)

CONTENT（内容）　　　　1　　　2　　　3　　　4　　　5

Comment: (　　　　　　　　　　　　　　　　　　　　　)

------ ✄ 切り取り ✄ ------

Date (　　　/　　　) PRESENTATION GROUP (No.　　) 得点　　　/10

DELIVERY（発表者の様子）　**Weak**　　　　**Average**　　　　**Great**

　　　　　　　　　　　　　1　　　2　　　3　　　4　　　5

Comment: (　　　　　　　　　　　　　　　　　　　　　)

CONTENT（内容）　　　　1　　　2　　　3　　　4　　　5

Comment: (　　　　　　　　　　　　　　　　　　　　　)

------ ✄ 切り取り ✄ ------

Date (　　　/　　　) PRESENTATION GROUP (No.　　) 得点　　　/10

DELIVERY（発表者の様子）　**Weak**　　　　**Average**　　　　**Great**

　　　　　　　　　　　　　1　　　2　　　3　　　4　　　5

Comment: (　　　　　　　　　　　　　　　　　　　　　)

CONTENT（内容）　　　　1　　　2　　　3　　　4　　　5

Comment: (　　　　　　　　　　　　　　　　　　　　　)

------ ✄ 切り取り ✄ ------

name :

name :

name :

name :

name :

name :

Useful Expressions for Presentation

I'd like to point out that ~	～という事を指摘したい
The question is how we should ~	問題は私たちがいかに～すべきかだ
~ match one's needs best	～のニーズに合う
It's really indispensable for us to ~	～することが本当に不可欠である
These facts show ~	これらの事実から～が分かる
In my opinion ~	私の意見としては、～
I personally think that ~	個人的に～だと思う
I'm in favor of ~	～に賛成である
To what degree do you think ~ realistic?	～はどの程度現実的だと思いますか？
I will give you an overview of ~	～について概略を述べます
I am going to talk about the status of ~	～の状況について話します
I support the idea of ~	～の考えを支持する
~ has more advantages than disadvantages	～はマイナス面よりプラス面の方が多い
I can't support the idea because ~	私はその考えを支持できない。なぜなら～
The consensus is that ~	一致した意見は～である
There are advantages and disadvantages to~	～にはメリットとデメリットがある
We have to think about ~	～について考えなければならない
We have to be more careful dealing with~	～を取り扱うには、より注意を払う必要がある
As far as I'm concerned ~	私に関する限り～、私の考えでは～である
What I'd like to stress is that ~	私が強調したいのは～である
The best alternative is to ~	最善の代替案は～である
The fact is that ~	事実は～である
In a similar vein	同様に
When it comes to ~	～と言えば
The problem is that ~	問題は～である
In my view	私の意見では
One of the factors might be ~	要因の１つは～かもしれない
Without a doubt	疑いなく
Unfortunately, we are unable to ~	残念ながら、私たちは～することができない
It was due to ~	それは～が原因だった
Compared to the past	以前と比べると
The major obstacle is ~	重大な障害は～である
In my opinion, we should ~	私の意見では～すべきである
The next step is to deal with ~	次のステップは～に取り組むことである
I'm for the idea of ~	私は～という考えに賛成である
I'm against the idea of ~	私は～という考えに反対である
To summarize that point	その点を要約すると
be in charge of ~	～の責任者である
The underlying issue here is that ~	ここで根本的な問題は～である
Do you know ~?	～をご存じですか？
Have you ever heard about ~?	～についてお聞きになったことはありませんか？
Do you know anything about ~?	～について何かご存知でしょうか？
Today, I would like to talk to you about ~	今日は～についてお話ししたいと思います
I chose this topic because ~	私がこの話題を選んだ理由は～
In this talk, I will touch on three points.	今回私が話したいのは次の３つの点です。
First, I will tell you about ~	最初にお話ししたいのは～
Second, I will talk about ~	次にお話ししたいのは～
Third, I will make several proposals that I think could help to solve these problems.	３番目に、これらの問題を解決するのに役立ついくつかの提案をしたいと思います。

Thank you for listening. Now I would like to respond to your questions or comments.	ご静聴ありがとうございました。さて、皆様からの質問やコメントに答えたいと思います。
The reason why I chose this topic is that ~	この話題を選んだ理由は～
I would like to give you my reasons.	私なりの理由をあげてみます。
There are (three) reasons why I disagree.	私が反対であるのには（3つの）理由があります。
I have (three) reasons why I think so.	私がそう考えるには（3つの）理由があります。
In concluding, I should note that ~	結論として～と述べておきたい。
Finally, it seems appropriate to remark that ~	最後に、～ということを指摘しておくことが妥当だ。
Thank you for your presentation. I was especially happy to hear that ~. Now I have a question to ask.	ご発表ありがとうございました。～を伺い、特にうれしく思いました。さて質問があります。
If I may ask a question, what do you mean by ~?	～がどういう意味なのか、お伺いしたいのですが？
If I may ask a question, what do you mean by that statement?	そのお話しがどういう意味なのか、お伺いしたいのですが？
Would you clarify your last point?	最後の1点を説明していただけますか？
This is an extremely (= very) difficult question to answer.	お答えするのに非常に難しい質問です
As for your (first) question, I should say that ~	あなたの（第1の）質問について、私は～と言いたい
Would you please repeat the question?	もう一度ご質問をお願いします。
I would like to have your (second) question repeated? I didn't really understand it.	あなたの（2番目の）質問を繰り返していただけませんか？　よくわかりませんでした。
All in all, what was the result of your presentation?	結局、今回のご発表にはどういう成果があったのでしょうか？
What do you think are the best procedures for solving the problem?	問題の解決には、どのような方法が最善とお考えですか？
What procedures (ways) do you recommend?	どのような方法がよいと思いますか？
Have you made any comparison of your conclusion with ~ yet?	あなたの結論と～とを比較なさっていますか？
How do your results compare with the theory?	結果を理論と比べると、どうなりますか？
In the end, are the results consistent with the theory?	結果は理論と一致しましたか？

first	まず第1に	compared to ~	～に比較すれば
at first	最初に	similarly	同様に（類似したものとして）
first of all	まず最初に		
to begin with	はじめに	in the same way	同じように
in the end	終わりに	likewise	同じように
finally	最後に	on the other hand	他方で
lastly	最後に	on the contrary	対照的に
moreover	さらに	however	しかしながら
besides	その上に	nevertheless	しかしながら
in addition	加えて	incidentally	付随的に、ちなみに
furthermore	さらに	by the way	ところで
in comparison	比較すれば、それと比較して	for this reason	この理由のために
		that is why	こういうわけで
in comparison to ~	～と比較して		
in contrast	対照的に		